Jimmy —
Xmas 1958,
Frank.

The Gay Twenties

A DECADE OF THE THEATRE

GERTRUDE LAWRENCE

The
Gay Twenties

A Decade of the Theatre

Words by
J. C. TREWIN

Pictures by
RAYMOND MANDER & JOE MITCHENSON

Foreword by
NOËL COWARD

MACDONALD : LONDON

*A complete index of the contents and illustrations
of this book will be found on page 125.*

*First published in 1958 by
Macdonald & Co. (Publishers), Ltd.
16 Maddox Street, W.1
Made and printed in Great Britain by
Purnell & Sons, Ltd.
Paulton (Somerset) and London*

Foreword

BY NOËL COWARD

All that I would have liked to say in this brief foreword; all the apt comparisons between then and now; the flashes of nostalgic reminiscence; the tender and loving tributes to the dead and gone; all these have been written, and very well written, in the actual text of this book. In association with John Trewin, Raymond Mander and Joe Mitchenson, whose genius for esoteric research is by now well known, have covered the decade of the Twenties in the Theatre with, to me, exasperating thoroughness; exasperating because it leaves me with very little to write about, even myself, for I have been more than generously dealt with, not only in these pages but also in the *Theatrical Companion To Coward* by Raymond Mander and Joe Mitchenson, price three guineas, handsomely bound and obtainable at your nearest bookseller's. Send your order now.

I am reminded of a ghastly moment many years ago when I had been persuaded, bitterly against my will, to make an appeal at a grandiose banquet in aid of a most worthy charity. I was then, and am still, curiously intimidated by the thought of making impromptu speeches. This, although few people believe it, is true. Later years of experience have inured me to it a little, but I still feel that deathly chill of nerves, that onset of panic, when I am suddenly called upon to propose a toast or to say a graceful, and inevitably witty, Thank You for being placed in the position of honoured guest. On that far-off evening in the late Twenties I had made a fatal mistake. Being accustomed only to saying words that I had learnt and meticulously rehearsed, I composed an elaborate speech based mainly on the brochure published by the charity in question, and learned it word for word. I also practised it in front of a mirror until all the spontaneous hesitations and casual witticisms were as smooth as butter. Unfortunately, however, my appeal came last and was preceded by those of the Chairman, The Duke of Sutherland; the Patron, His Royal Highness The Duke of Gloucester, and the late Sir Patrick Hastings. As I sat, in a cold sweat, listening to them, I realised only too clearly that they too had

had a careful look at that damned brochure. By the time they had finished they had covered, between them, every single point in my speech, and I rose miserably to my feet with my eyes glazed, my mouth dry, and nothing to say whatever. I would like to be able to report that a miracle happened and that I talked in a scintillating manner for twenty minutes and was the success of the evening; this, however, would be untrue. I think I managed to utter a few clichés and get a couple of irrelevant laughs, but the applause when I sat down, although friendly, was muted.

Now I find myself in much the same dilemma, without of course the immediate sense of panic. I am at least alone and can, if necessary, tear up what I have written and start again or, at worst, send Mander and Mitchenson a cable saying that owing to various commitments I am unable to keep my promise to them. This, however, would be weak and unprincipled; and although I have indeed a great many other commitments, I shall press on and do the best I can.

On reading this book I was amused, but not surprised, to discover that I am still, and probably for ever will be, incurably stage-struck. The photographs alone evoke a flood of sentimental memories, not only because many of them are of people I knew and loved and will never see again, but also because they conjure up so clearly those challenging and, for me, remarkable years. Whether or not I was any happier then than I am now I cannot decide; in any case it is beside the point. Happiness *per se* was not, after all, the object of the enterprise.

The object of the enterprise for me then was to be a "success"—a triumphant, inverted-comma'd, name-in-lights success—and, lo and behold, after a few setbacks I achieved it. What is more—hold on to your hats, dear readers, and be prepared for a strange revelation—the Bitch Goddess was sweet to me when she came; she neither disillusioned me nor embittered me. She was warm and soothing and reassuring, and I loved her as I love her now, for, odd as it may seem and in spite of journalistic rumours to the contrary, we still occasionally meet. If and when she chooses to leave me I shall not repine, nor shall I mourn her any more than I mourn other loved ones who have gone away. I do not approve of mourning, I only approve of remembering, and her I shall always remember gratefully and with pride.

Between 1920 and 1930 I achieved a great deal of what I had set out to achieve and a great deal that I had not. I had not, for instance, envisaged in those early days of the Twenties that before the decade was over I would be laid low by a serious nervous breakdown, recover from it, and return to London to be booed off the stage and spat at in the streets. Nor did I imagine, faced by this unmannerly disaster, that only a few months would ensue before I would be back again, steadier and a great deal more triumphant than before.

The Twenties began for me with *"I'll Leave It To You"*, *The Young Idea*, *London Calling!*, *The Vortex*, *Fallen Angels*, *On With The Dance* and *Hay Fever*.

The decade ended for me with *Easy Virtue*, *The Queen Was In The Parlour*, *This Was A Man*, *Home Chat*, *Sirocco*, *This Year Of Grace!* and *Bitter-Sweet*.

Perhaps, after all, I am a suitable choice to write a foreword to this most engaging history of our Theatre in the Twenties. I cannot think off-hand of anyone who was more intimately and turbulently connected with it.

ACKNOWLEDGMENTS

Pictorially, the Twenties are covered mainly by the work of the now non-existent photographers, Foulsham and Banfield and The Stage Photo Company, but the work of the following, among others, has been included:

Bassano, 46 and 47; Lenare, 59, 78, 85, 102, 104, 106 and 114; Bertram Park, 8, 53 and 72; Sasha, *Frontispiece*, 54, 86, 90, 120, 126 and 128.

We are grateful to Frances Fleetwood for compiling an exhaustive index to the text and captions.

FOR WENDY

and

FOR PETER PAN

I

The Twenties were at least as gay as the Thirties would be overcast. Storms
may have battered them, alarums deafened them, governments crumpled
round them. But, at this remove, the word must be gay. In the middle
of the decade the song was "I want to be happy". At journey's end it was
"Spread a little happiness". Elsewhere: well, when the man that you care
for takes care of you, you'll be happy, and therefore—*he'll* be happy too.

The decade opened hard upon the beginning of the hyphen between
the wars. Few yet thought seriously of another war; the world, in recovery,
was expanding; there were changes in life and manners that would have
seemed crazy during the long early summer of 1914. Naturally the theatre
reflected this age of relaxed conventions, of fervid good cheer and questing
experiment. It was a decade ever ready to look at the new thing, to open
astonished and delighted eyes at any fresh idea, and at the same time to be
just as delighted if an old idea were suitably dressed up.

There were contradiction and paradox; fashions cancelled each other out;
experiment could become as wild as cakes-and-ale mirth could grow desperate.
At one limit we had, as A. G. Macdonell has said, plays of Illusionist Symbolism set throughout in the gallery of a salt-mine in Upper Silesia. At the
other limit, those Bright Young People wore their hectic flush (an old epithet
newly applied). All said, it remained the gay Twenties: the chaotic Twenties,
if you wish; not a restful decade, but one—and the songs people sing can
speak for themselves—that ran to a jaunty rhythm:

> Say, guys,
> I'm puttin' you wise,
> You can't have my Sugar for tea.

Restless years, then, and, in retrospect, with a strange wistfulness under
the gaiety; a theatrical decade, too, that sustained rightly a Theatre Theatrical.

Its voices are those of Noël Coward, wittily casual or resolutely sincere; Tallulah Bankhead, all smoky syrup, dahling; Leslie Henson, the tones of a husky goldfish; Edith Day, a romantic soprano—O Rose Marie, we loved you! Jack Buchanan and the Astaires danced for the Twenties; the Co-Optimists fooled for them. Charles B. Cochran was their impresario. Their symbol, that mingling of gaminerie and grace, was Gertrude Lawrence, born under her dancing star. James Agate wrote of her in *Oh, Kay!*: "She will take up a doll, and, by holding it to her breast and crooning to it, take you straight into the infantile heart of woman, and in the next moment, holding the wretched thing by the ankle, plunge you into a world of mockery from which sentiment and sentimentality have been banished." And Noël Coward has said, simply: "Gertrude Lawrence, of all the actresses I know, could, when she was playing true, give me the most pleasure."

These were the gayer Twenties. It was a world, also, of the romantic actor, though not now in the uniform, green with gold frogs, of Princess Sonia's Hussars, a regiment that the war had dispersed to the deeper provinces and *His Midnight Bride*. Even more, it was a world of the naturalism long personified by Gerald du Maurier, whose carefully careless manner, calculated to each tap of the cigarette upon its case, was bred of an intricate technique. It was, and oddly, a world in which great acting flowered, in which Sybil Thorndike could apostrophise the towers of burning Troy, or face her judges in the hall at Rouen, and in which Edith Evans's Millamant, voice of the Restoration, entered St. James's Park, fan spread and streamers out, crying: "Lord, have I not made violent haste? . . . I have enquired after you, as after a new fashion."

New York with its stage in sudden gaudy blossom after years pitiably arid, sent play upon play, good, moderate, appalling, until somebody christened London Broadway-on-Thames. The thriller, a word dire but inevitable, had its panel-creaking hour. There were plays as contentious as *The Vortex* and *The Fanatics*, each as much of a tempest in its day as *Look Back in Anger* would be in the Fifties; as "shocking" as Hopwood's *The Garden of Eden*, with its tossed-off wedding dress; as gentle as the purring romance of *Marigold*. Shaw was writing at his height; Galsworthy stood for the purposeful play; Maugham added his astringency; Coward, theatrical spirit of his time, knew better than anyone the rules of give-and-take repartee, "Brief, short, quick, snap"; Barrie moved towards the moon in wavering morrice; Lonsdale moved from Duke to Duke, Drinkwater examined the great commoners; and O'Casey, Dublin genius in a Fair Isle jumper, found again the Elizabethan union of tragedy and farce, that prodigal bounty of words in torchlight procession.

The Aldwych farces, children of the Twenties, were in dizzying whirl. Musical comedy glittered and flashed. Ballet dancers, Russian and English, were shaping the modern history of another art. The Gate Theatre Studio raised its cheap sacking curtain in a Floral Street attic. Cabaret tinkled by the midnight tables. How can we hope to pin with a single adjective this chaotic, fermenting, uncertain decade? Seen now from a distance, it is still a little more than life-sized. The colours glisten, much of the gilt is not yet tarnished, the eagerness lingers. It makes violent haste. It enquires always after a new fashion.

At last, no longer unchallenged, the high-pitched years of war behind it, and receding, the theatre of the Twenties had to face the cinema. By the end of the period the screen would be talking, and the theatre would have to talk back more urgently, laugh louder, dance more furiously. But by then, by the Thirties, the laughter was growing sour, the zest forced. A jaded theatre moved towards 1939. Our story must linger in the rebellious Twenties —at their zenith, hopeful, excited, gay. Gay is the word. It will serve, whether the voice is that of

> I'll be back inside a minute
> With a taxi—you'll be in it,
> And we'll seek some cosy place in which to dine

or, warningly, of Coward's

> Though you're only seventeen,
> Far too much of life you've seen,
> Syncopated child! . . .

II

1920

We can call 1920 the Wayward Year: one without the slightest sense of direction. Its record is "like a tangled chain; nothing impair'd but all disorder'd". As good a place as any to start is at the beginning, and we find that the decade opened to the mildest of zephyrs—stroked in by A. A. Milne's *Mr. Pim Passes By*, produced at the New Theatre on January 5, 1920. This has passed by so often, and on so many stages (and has now itself, I fear, been by-passed) that it is hard to imagine the house at that cheerful première, enraptured by Olivia and her everlasting curtains, and by the tones of Mr. Pim, wavering in with his mind of uncarded wool. His Christian name was Carraway: a warning, no doubt, that Milne was a whimsical dramatist. True, but he was also an amusing one. His wit, civilised and gentle—for he had no cruelty in him—derived from the *Punch* of his day; in the french-window frivolities of light comedy, all roses and racquets, he had no match.

Grace before meat, doubtless; but *Mr. Pim* is the kind of piece, good-tempered, good-hearted, that must jolt any amateur dramatist hoping to copy it. Not that, in these days, anyone would be likely to try. It is, firmly, a period exhibit. Everything rests upon Pim's form of aphasia. He gets the wife of a county magistrate to believe that she has committed bigamy, though anyone might be forgiven for muddling the names of Jacob Telworthy (who was Olivia's first husband) and of Ernest Polwittle (presumably a scandalous Cornishman). What could be more alike? Pim was a passing part that the producer and actor, Dion Boucicault, loved; but the play rested upon Boucicault's wife, Irene Vanbrugh, whose mannerism of keeping her eyes lowered and glancing up suddenly with a glint of demure domestic mischief was familiar in fifty English comedies.

Mr. Pim had soon to be transferred from the New because Matheson Lang arrived in February with a melodrama called *Carnival*, which he and

H. C. M. Hardinge had taken from the Italian *Sirocco*. Lang, handsome and sonorous, was the most consistent romantic player of the Twenties, an actor who never seemed really at ease in a lounge suit, though he wore one in parts of *Carnival*. There he appeared as an Italian tragedian who was Othello both on the stage and in his private life. Matheson Lang never patronised his characters. He enjoyed them and presented them sincerely in the broad romantic method, a confident technique that derived from his early years with Benson and that kept him at the head of his own branch of the profession. *Carnival* was a florid play, but he believed in it in the theatre, almost as much as in *Othello* itself, which he put on for matinées—overlooked at first—that made many wish he had kept steadily to Shakespeare.

While he was off in the provinces after *Carnival*, getting a new melodrama ready, a very light comedy indeed, by an actor-dramatist, slipped into the New Theatre without any kind of parade. It was called *"I'll Leave it to You,"* and its programme to-day is valuable. The author, who acted in the play himself, with great enjoyment though his performance would not trouble posterity, was Noël Coward, then aged twenty. Gilbert Miller had supplied the title and the idea. When it arrived in London, but not now under Miller's management, its first night hurtled to success. The run, alas, did not match the reception. To-day the little piece can still come from the text with a brisk flourish, especially the part of Uncle Dan (played at the New by E. Holman Clark), who had a mission in life, apparently a fortune to bequeath, a variety of nephews and nieces, and a gift for prevarication.

Exactly a month of these events at Mulberry Manor was enough for the London run. Then Lang swooped back to the New with a sad piece of tushery entitled *The Wandering Jew* (by E. Temple Thurston), which he staged and performed with as much care and respect as if it had been *Lear*. This determined drama was written in smears of grease-paint, in prose always on the splinter-edge of bad verse ("I'll sift this matter to what end I can"), but its passage through the centuries, from Jerusalem to Antioch, Palermo, and Seville, made a romantic scenic-railway excursion that was accepted at once with the right theatrical awe, and it went on running for 390 performances (with revivals to come). Lang was burned at the stake every night, a most satisfying illusion, achieved very simply with flutters of red and yellow silk, suitable lights, and some smoking asthma powder:

Matteo's garments can be seen to get slowly black. His head is still thrown back meeting the light as the flames leap up against him. At last, when all his garment is charred and the skin of his face discoloured, the light goes out, and his head falls forward on his chest.

It was during the first London run of *The Wandering Jew* that Mrs. Patrick Campbell came round to see Lang, one night after his burning, and said in her deep velvet voice: "Mr. Matheson Lang, I have never heard of you before—but I would like to act with you." The scorched actor took it well, but unfortunately what might have been a tumultuous partnership never came about.

The more generous romantics had good fun this year. Musical comedy had not yet chartered the great stage of Drury Lane (though pantomime kept its traditional bravery). Instead, everyone had to go to the Mary Anderson-Robert Hichens version of *The Garden of Allah*, weeping like anything to see such quantities of sand. The part-author, Mary Anderson de Navarro, once a famous actress, thought it was done much better in New York. She was dismayed to find Arthur Collins, the Drury Lane director, making Saharan "stars" by cutting slits in the sky-cloth ("On the first night the stars burst out like a rash on the face of heaven"), and the sandstorm, which was one of the news stories of the day, also disappointed her. It became a news story because, on the first night, the sand, actually pea-flour, billowed over the footlights—there had been a protective gauze at rehearsal—and peppered the front stalls until their elaborately-dressed occupants were miller-white.

Still, the melodrama ("Peace and even happiness are only to be found in self-sacrifice") delighted its audience, from gallery to orchestra-rail. Godfrey Tearle, as the young Trappist who broke his priestly vows to find love—in the person of Madge Titheradge—in a Saharan oasis, had one of the year's romantic orgies. "The part is full of opportunities for declamatory display," said a critic with enthusiasm. He was right. *The Garden of Allah* was what cinema publicists would have called a colourful epic. They would probably have worked in "nostalgic" as well, if that had been a vogue-word in the Twenties.

Nobody can now look back, wistfully, at the record of 1920, and, without foreknowledge, say that the London stage was moving in any special

direction. The reign of the actor-manager was practically over. Sir John
Martin Harvey had said glumly: "We have no one who will sacrifice himself
for the benefit of the higher drama in London by maintaining on his own
shoulders the great traditions of the past."

Even so, plenty was happening. London offered its romantic melodramas. It offered a topical drama (that has endured) by John Galsworthy
and another (that has not) by a young writer, Ernest Hutchinson, who died
in the following year. *The Right to Strike*, as Hutchinson called his play, had
a theme that Galsworthy would have admired, and that would be relevant
to-day. From provincial repertory during the late Twenties, I remember
yet a moment when the Lancashire doctors of Valleyhead struck in protest
at the strike of railwaymen. It was this that caused the Garrick Theatre
gallery to boo furiously midway through the first night, though all ended in
general applause.

What else in the London list? There were several frivolous comedies,
with such personages as the Earl of Knightsbridge and Lord Sloane (*Brown
Sugar*), and with cap-and-apron fun in the servants' hall (*Come Out of the
Kitchen* from America). *His Lady Friends*, a Broadway dramatisation of an
English novel, had characters that would arrive again presently in a famous
musical comedy, *No, No, Nanette*. (Similarly, *A Pair of Sixes*, lost in the run-
of-the-mill during 1920, would reappear later as the musical *Queen High*.) A
war-time farce, *French Leave*, with a purplish Brigadier-General and a mademoiselle from Armentières, volleyed and thundered: its author, Reginald
Berkeley, would write more seriously about a war that was still too near to
bring to the stage.

Such intimate revues as *Jumble Sale* and *Just Fancy*, put on at the Vaudeville by the inventive André Charlot, now give to us nothing but their titles,
and not much then. Rough-cast melodrama had its audience, and *Boy of
my Heart* (with such characters as Detective Thorne and A Red-haired Woman)
ran at the Lyceum. A few unsensational detective plays—no panels in *At
the Villa Rose*, with Arthur Bourchier as the bland Hanaud—a first tremor of
Grand Guignol at the tiny Little, a certain amount of Shakespeare (with
Ainley singing "O Julius C. was an N.U.T." when taking a first-night call
at the St. James's), a Roman tragedy by Masefield, a fantasy by Barrie,
Charles B. Cochran at the Pavilion, *The Beggar's Opera* in remote Hammersmith: no special pattern here. It does not help to recall an Australian

domestic comedy (a failure) entitled *On Our Selection*, a far, lost ancestor of *The Summer of the Seventeenth Doll*.

Musical comedies were long, lush, wholly unselfconscious. In an Alhambra revue, *Johnny Jones and his Sister Sue*, the ripely dignified George Robey went on "a sort of Cook's tour", appearing now as Louis XV, now as a dervish in danger of treading on his twenty-year-old beard. Out in the New Cut Lilian Baylis was very slowly shaping what had been a kind of South London Mission, a coffee-and-culture settlement, into the ultimate splendours of the Old Vic. Clearly any student of what we have now to call "trends" would have applied an ice-pack and retired.

In those days the student would have much ground to cover. He would have flickered, a well-meaning Carraway Pim, round such theatres, since vanished, as the Alhambra, Daly's, the Empire, the Gaiety, the Holborn Empire (matinées of *The Trojan Women* and *Medea*: at night, Harry Tate), the Kennington, the Kingsway, the Little, the London Pavilion, the Lyceum, New Oxford, the Playhouse, the Royalty, the Shaftesbury, the St. James's, the Surrey. He would not have troubled to go to His Majesty's, unless he was a Saturday-night regular, because *Chu-Chin-Chow* (Cobbler's Song, camels, and all) had been running there since August 31, 1916: a production, lavishly moonstruck, with the Arabian Nights behind it, that had become a London habit: nougat, but to most people (the late Sir Herbert Tree excepted) palatable nougat. On the first night a rival producer had prophesied a run of six weeks.

Chu-Chin-Chow, though its endurance record has yielded (as I write in the early summer of 1958) to Agatha Christie's *The Mousetrap* at a much smaller theatre, lingers in stage history simply for the persistence of its run. It may be useful, looking back over forty years, to see what else is generally recalled, and why. At random, a wisp by Gertrude Jennings, *The Young Person in Pink*: its name has preserved it, and its opening scene in Hyde Park. Otherwise, it is known to collectors because women in the cast outnumbered the men by twelve to two, and because the endeared Sydney Fairbrother, who had played in *Chu* for three-and-a-half years—and when saved, she said, was on the edge of gibbering—welcomed the chance to create "a lovely old scoundrel" called Mrs. Badger.

Somerset Maugham's *The Unknown* is remembered because the bereaved mother (Haidée Wright), her sons killed in the war, said: "Who is going to

1. *The Young Person in Pink* at the Haymarket Theatre, 1920: Joyce Carey exclaims to Ellis Jeffreys, "Mother! Mother! I have found you!" to the consternation of Gladys Calthrop, Ormonde Wynne, Sybil Carlisle, Mary Barton, and Donald Calthrop.

2. Journey to Holyhead: The railway compartment scene in *Paddy the Next Best Thing*, Savoy Theatre, 1920, with Ion Swinley, Peggy O'Neil (in the title-role), and Winifred Evans. The journey was repeated on 867 occasions.

3. Godfrey Tearle, as the renegade monk, is consoled by Madge Titheradge in the Saharan scene of *The Garden of Allah* at the Theatre Royal, Drury Lane, in 1920.

4. "Dick grew to manhood, and Emmeline became the most beautiful thing on the island." Faith Celli and Harold French in *The Blue Lagoon*, Prince of Wales's, 1920.

5. *Mary Rose*, Haymarket Theatre, 1920: Leon Quartermaine, Fay Compton, and Ernest Thesiger on the Isle-that-likes-to-be-visited in the first production of Barrie's fantasy which ran for 399 performances.

6. The young people (Georgette Cohan and Leslie Howard) in *Mr. Pim Passes By* at the New Theatre, 1920, are ready to offer advice in an awkward predicament. Their elders are Ethel Griffies, Ben Webster, and Irene Vanbrugh.

7. Matheson Lang, shocked by the appearance of Hilda Bayley in her Bacchante costume in *Carnival* (New Theatre, 1920), demands: "Simonetta! What are you?"

8. Sybil Thorndike in an unlikely character. She was called Carmen, and the play in which she appeared was the Grand Guignol *G.H.Q. Love* at the Little Theatre, 1920.

9. *The Truth About the Russian Dancers* as told by J. M. Barrie with the aid of Tamara Karsavina and Basil Foster in a variety bill at the London Coliseum in 1920.

10. José Collins as Dolores in *A Southern Maid* (Daly's, 1920), of which James Agate said: "As between this play and its predecessor, *The Maid of the Mountains*, there is plenty of resemblance but no essential difference."

11. Polly (Sylvia Nelis) sings "Fondly let me loll!" to Macheath (Frederick Ranalow) in *The Beggar's Opera* at the Lyric Theatre, Hammersmith, 1920.

forgive God?" H. M. Harwood's political drama, *The Grain of Mustard Seed*, and Lennox Robinson's Irish comedy, *The White-headed Boy*, were plays that later bore revival. Stage versions of Stacpoole's *The Blue Lagoon* and of the sicklier *Paddy, the Next Best Thing* pleased playgoers—and these must always be ready—who liked to see popular novels translated to the theatre. To-day little can be quite so theatrically flat as the grass-skirt and coral-island romp of the first play, or the darling Oirish hoyden of the second, a curious visitor in the era of the "troubles". *Paddy* now is thought of less for the acting of the arch-ingénue, Peggy O'Neil, than for a scene in a railway compartment, with hoyden and friend bound for Holyhead. The British theatre has always enjoyed playing with trains: we shall meet another example later in the decade.

Most of the London plays would go out to the provinces, then bristling with theatres (as fine as the Ionic-columned Royal at Plymouth) and entwined in tours, numbers One, Two, Three, even farther: fourteen companies at one time were out with *The Maid of the Mountains*. In 1920 the strolling player had not to meet the full drive of the cinema. And besides the touring theatres, there were the oldest of the repertory companies: Barry Jackson's at Birmingham ("the captive image of a dream"); the Liverpool Playhouse; George S. King's pocket "Rep" at Plymouth that would live long in the memory of the South-west.

The music-hall was in jubilant voice, even if hybrid, draggle-tail revues were beginning to occupy too many stages; and the old melodrama men still fought. You could have sat, more or less enthralled, at *A Broken Butterfly* (New, Pontypridd), *The Daughter of a Thief* (Grand, Halifax), *The Gentleman from Dartmoor* (Royal, Leicester), *Should a Husband Forgive?* (Grand, Aberaman), or—nearer London, and very simply—at *Shame* (Royal, Stratford). That was Stratford-atte-Bowe. By the Avon, W. Bridges-Adams was producing Shakespeare with uncommon clarity and speed in the old pinnacled and turreted red-brick Memorial Theatre, architecturally Early Marzipan.

Certain plays of 1920 live now for their disasters. Probably we should never think of *The Mayflower*, at the old Surrey, if it were not that a property vessel about to sail from Plymouth capsized when (said W. A. Darlington) it was "in full sail for the wings", and scattered its Pilgrim Fathers in heaps upon the stage. The first line of the next scene was "Let us give thanks to God who hath brought us safely across the ocean": the audience responded

B

to it. Another piece, *One Night in Rome*, by J. Hartley Manners—in which the dramatist's wife, Laurette Taylor, acted at the Garrick—lives because of the first-night riot during which pennies were tossed upon the stage, and stink-bombs and electric snuff thrown into the stalls. It was assumed at first that people in the gallery had protested because, with an opening set upon which the curtain had been raised to only one-third of its usual height, they could not see more than a few feet of the stage. But these people, with a legitimate grievance none realised until the play began, would not have brought their ammunition to the Garrick. Later, and more plausibly, someone suggested that an Australian, whose "girl friend" wanted Laurette Taylor's part, had paid a gang to create the disturbance.

Charles B. Cochran, pink-faced, pale-eyed, and courteous, the master-showman who presented the play—at two "first" nights—had a variety of failures that year, *One Night in Rome* among them. His revue, *London, Paris, and New York*, on the small stage of the Pavilion, was prosperous enough, and marked by the idiosyncratic style and taste, and the gift for what was called spectacular intimacy, that always stamped a Cochran production. This, written by Arthur Wimperis, was Cochran's first important work at the "Pav" without the French comedienne Delysia, for London the spirit of Paris. A young girl who used only her Christian name, June, sang a duet with the fantastic chameleon, Nelson Keys ("Bunch"), whose evening's work included a German bandsman, a Spanish brigand, a Cockney tipster, Henry Ainley, a Japanese juggler (the management had to pay £42 for false teeth), and a bunch of other characters, few of them remotely like Keys. Later in the run Cochran introduced a pair of American dancers, Carl Hyson and the drift of thistledown that was London's first sight of Dorothy Dickson. He also brought in, at various times, Violet Loraine, in her last appearance before her marriage, and, of all things—though the Parisian label justified it—a scene from *Andromaque*, with Edouard de Max, from the Comédie Française, in the madness of Orestes.

These matters alone should be enough to ensure remembrance of *London, Paris, and New York*; but the revue is the most ephemeral of forms. A modish production can command the town while it runs, but, as soon as the theatre is dark again, the revue is likely to slip into oblivion with the evening newspaper of the night before. It is surprising how soon the complex elaborations wane, how numbers from one revue blend and blur in the mind with others long past. Probably only the Coward and Herbert Farjeon revues have now any marked identity of their own.

I have spoken of the decade as gaily chaotic, and I repeat that 1920 was a chaotic year, resisting any attempt to impose artificial order upon it. Let me say, quickly, that in straight drama playgoers went round talking of Galsworthy's *The Skin Game* at the St. Martin's, still London's newest theatre. This fine play, its author's first commercial success, dramatised a battle between the Hillcrists and the invading Hornblowers, the county's old order and the blatant new-rich manufacturers. Shamelessly, Mrs. Hillcrist ignores the rules of the game to get the Hornblowers out of Deepwater. With its famous curtain-line, "What's gentility worth if it can't stand fire?" (spoken by Athole Stewart), *The Skin Game* was strong Galsworthian hammer-and-tongs, exhilarating yet in performance, though in 1958 we can meet the most latterly neglected of all dramatists only on the television screen. (Considered in terms of the available audience for one night of television, this may not be regarded as neglect.) Helen Haye and Athole Stewart acted the Hillcrists for Basil Dean, with Edmund Gwenn to defy them. Nowadays the eye halts suddenly at the name of Meggie Albanesi, legend among young actresses, who had just begun to fulfil herself in the exciting productions of the Reandean management.

It would have much surprised the early Twenties to know that one day Galsworthy would be out of fashion. They would have been horrified (and incredulous also), to hear that, *Peter Pan* apart, Barrie would be with him, mute on the shelf. Barrie's *Mary Rose* had been offered to, and refused—though unwillingly—by the acknowledged leader of the stage, Gerald du Maurier, who would spend much of this year as a peculiarly dashing French-man in a forgotten comedy, *The Prude's Fall*.

In *Mary Rose* he would have doubled father and son in a ghost-play about a girl who vanished on a Hebridean island that "likes to be visited". There were uncomfortable passages when Barrie let his whimsicality wander. Others had a strange, shivering beauty: now and then we felt the same *frisson*, the same helpless terror that marked the end of the second act of *Dear Brutus*. The play, with Fay Compton's Mary Rose, trembled at once into success: it had something in it to console many whom the war had bereaved. Now it may choke the cynical. Listeners have to choose for themselves which side they are on when they hear the key line, "The loveliest time will be when my baby is a man and takes me on his knee, instead of me taking him on mine."

Barrie this year wrote an odd little one-act play for Tamara Karsavina and christened it, topically, *The Truth About the Russian Dancers*. It was done at the Coliseum, and rightly, because Diaghilev's ballet had appeared so often at that theatre, in Fokine's *Cléopâtre*, with its burning colours, in *The Good-Humoured Ladies*, *Schéhérazade*, a dozen other fiercely-relished excitements. It would be some years before Arnold Haskell coined the word "balletomane", and though Diaghilev's dancers had many rapturous devotees, people could still think of the art as Max Beerbohm had in 1906 ("Ballet not merely gives me no illusion; it conveys no meaning to me"), or as James Agate would in 1943: "How the same twiddle can express both chalk and cheese will ever remain beyond my comprehension". Never mind: Barrie was an admirer, and a powerful one. He must have made at least ten drafts of his *Russian Dancers*, "showing how they marry, how they are made, with how they die and live happily ever afterwards". It delighted more than the ballet fanatics (those who remembered, in Farjeon's words of a later day, "how Bolonsky danced *Belushka* in September 1910"), when Karsavina, at the Coliseum, danced through her lines, executing six pirouettes when she kissed the mother of her betrothed. On she went, nursing her baby, dying, rising to dance ("dead Russian dancers do"), and so forward, fantastically, in the kind of life and death that none but Barrie could have known that Russian dancers lived and died. He was perfectly sure of it himself.

I have quoted Max Beerbohm. This quietest, deadliest of critics—who became, so oddly, a lamb-like myth in old age—recurs when we reach Grand Guignol. He heartily disliked the French Grand Guignol company when it came to London in 1908: "Horror for horror's sake offends me. I do not say that I always shun it; merely that I am rightly ashamed of yielding to it." And he said in the course of his essay: "It does seem to me a matter for congratulation that native equivalents for such plays as *L'Angoisse* could not possibly become popular in London."

What, if anything, he added, twelve years later from his retirement in Italy, I do not know; but certainly the Grand Guignol plays, in English variation, became vastly popular at the Little. Audiences in the Gay Twenties that would weep at *Mary Rose*—Barrie had himself something of the torturer's quality—or laugh at *Mr. Pim*, or debate *The Skin Game* hotly, or blink at the human transformation scene that was Nelson Keys, would go also to be chilled at the Guignol.

Sure enough, *L'Angoisse*, in an English version as *The Medium*, was among the plays, and Sybil Thorndike, the young emotional actress of Euripides and Shakespeare, who was regarded as one of the hopes of the British theatre, appeared in it, encased in plaster. It was one of twenty-five parts that she acted with intense relish during the all-but-two years' run of the Guignol series. During 1920 the shocks were relatively mild; but honest citizens would have sterner stuff to come, though (as I have said) the ideal Guignol play is a nightmare that derives from Poe and Le Fanu, with footnotes by John Webster's Bosola in his cords-and-coffin manner. It rarely comes to us.

Sybil Thorndike, during the Guignol run, would go now and again to refresh herself with remote classical parts on Sunday nights at such a theatre as the Lyric, Hammersmith, a stage on which some of the producing societies, experimental and otherwise—they had begun now to swarm— found urbane hospitality. One of the dramas done there, the Stage Society's *Forerunners*, "a tragedy of the abstract past", was a prehistoric peep that must have been, unconsciously, a joy. (Sybil Thorndike was not in this.) We recall it for an agonised cry by Arnold Bennett in his *Journal*. An actor, he said, "introduced me to the author. I said to him: 'You have written a highly curious play.' Later I said: 'You have written a damned curious play.' This was the best I could do."

He could do, and did, a great deal more in praise of *The Beggar's Opera*, the production that re-burnished the name of John Gay, and that kept people coming out to darker Hammersmith, over the hills and far away, through a street market, past the whelks, and down a cul-de-sac, for nearly three years. (Once they had found the way to Hammersmith, they went on going throughout the decade.)

Bennett was a director of the Lyric, but the genius of the place was Nigel Playfair, whose highly selective, highly individual productions, with a style and zest entirely their own, set the Lyric firmly in the theatre of the Twenties: at heart, during the Playfair reign, it was usually a couple of centuries older. To-day the names of Gay and Playfair are, most properly, lettered in gold in the auditorium of the theatre that has reverted to its old name of Lyric Opera House, and that retains its decorations in what Playfair called "the best mid-Victorian rococo-revivalist style".

It is a very long stride indeed from the Lyric, Lovat Fraser's designs, and Frederick Ranalow singing "The Charge is Prepared" or "Before the Barn Door Crowing", to the commercial musical comedies of the year. If— as it has been asserted—a period is known by its musical-comedy stars, then 1920 did not differ much from the years before it. We find the usual list. There was *A Little Dutch Girl*, full of Crown Princes, Grand Duchesses, Dowager Duchesses, and Barons (Lauri de Frece as Baron Bomba). There was *A Southern Maid* at Daly's, with José Collins in flaming orange, and unmistakably from the right latitude, as more or less another maid of the mountains. (Off-stage she had a boudoir in *rose du Barri*.) At the Adelphi W. H. Berry frisked through *A Naughty Princess*—a highly curious play, Arnold Bennett might have said—as King Michael of Panoplia, with George Grossmith as Prince Ladislas. When Berry entered as the King, returning from a boar-hunt, he wore green tights, a green velvet tunic, and very high glacé hunting-boots, with a large crown stamped on each leg. "I've got a horse in my stable," he observed, "but as I'm broke there's only half-a-crown on that."

At the fashionable Winter Garden, its years as the "Old Mo" music-hall forgotten, Leslie Henson, of the crumpled-trout face, rocketed huskily through *A Night Out*, a wild adaptation of the Parisian farce we think of now as *Hotel Paradiso*; and in possibly the best-remembered of the musical plays, *Irene*, at the Empire, Edith Day was singing:

> Till it wilted I wore it,
> I'll always adore it,
> My sweet little Alice-blue gown.

A critic was to write warningly, when the play was revived a quarter of a century on: "Don't call her Ireenie, the name is I-reen; a waif who is shop-girl and musical queen." With dour resolution he rhymed on through his notice.

The tunes remain. It is what happens between the tunes that now disconcerts us. "Come on, girls," the leader of the chorus will cry at the end of so many first acts. "Let's all go on board the Prince's yacht," or "Let's all go to Transylvania":

> For we've all of us a mania
> To trot through Transylvania,
> To totter in the Transylvanian rain;
> So pick up your umbrella,
> Ev'ry girl and ev'ry fella,
> And travel by the Transylvanian train.
> Transylvanian puff-puff,
> Yours and mine,
> Transylvanian chuff-chuff,
> Whistle down the line . . .

That was the sort of preferred jingle, though most librettists did it better and showed no desire to fix their audiences all night in a pyjama factory or a baseball ground. It is not only facile wistfulness for the *pièces roses* of a lost land that makes some of their friends recall them. It was a theatrical world of preposterous and affectionately-accepted fantasy. The musical stage, as Daisy Ashford said of the palace, was "packed with men of a noble nature. . . . Dukes were as nought, as there were a good lot of princes and Arch Dukes as it was a very superier levie indeed".

I am justified in quoting Miss Ashford because in this year, 1920, *The Young Visitors* came itself to the stage: not with any special inspiration, but long enough for its devotees to meet Ethel Monticue, Mr. Salteena, the Earl of Clincham, and, of course, the Archduchess of Greenwich. "Well, now," announced the Prince, putting on his crown, "I have booked a valse with the Archduchess of Greenwich and this is her favourite tune."

III

1921

If 1920 had been a year of chaos, 1921 was the year of failures. More often than at any other time during the decade the gallery gave its own version of "the faint cold sound of the Morte". (This continues to be one of the less-gay aspects of first-night playgoing.) Even if not all of them were booed, nearly fifty productions of 1921 lasted for only a few days or weeks, and I doubt whether many people can now put the authors' names to *Hanky Panky John*, *The Ninth Earl*, *Two Jacks and a Jill*, *By All Means, Darling*, and *Araminta Arrives*. They vanished quickly enough, with dozens of others, struggling mayflies. One of these, a play, *M'Lady*, that lasted for twenty-three performances, was by Edgar Wallace: his hour in the theatre had not sounded. It seemed obvious this year that playgoers wanted strong drama, flamboyant comedy, or the kind of musical romance, amply-upholstered and with the Archduchess of Greenwich's favourite tune, that they had been used to for so long.

It was not yet a time for experiment. People went contentedly to John Street, Adelphi, to watch Sybil Thorndike having her eyes stabbed out by knitting needles in the lunatic ward of an asylum, being crushed with her lover beneath a movable ceiling, or seeing her husband tossed alive to the wolfhounds. They went to observe Matheson Lang as a bullfighter ("romantic," mused James Agate alarmingly, "only in the sense that the anthropophagi are romantic"), or as a Christopher Sly transformed to a poet-tinker with a tragic end. They went to see one of Bulldog Drummond's enemies tumble into an acid bath; to hear Charles Hawtrey of all people crying "Stap my vitals!"; to applaud W. H. Berry when he appeared at the Adelphi as a Duchess in a green sequin dress and ostrich plumes; or to laugh at George Robey, at the Alhambra, in the green velvet suit of the Millais "Bubbles".

24

12. Norah Blaney and Gwendoline Farrar contributors to both "the musical excellence and the gay repartee" of *Pot Luck*, Vaudeville, 1921.

13. Jennie and Rosie Dolly demurely showing a leg in *The League of Notions*, Cochran's revue at the New Oxford Theatre, 1921.

14. A famous dancing partnership: Dorothy Dickson and Carl Hyson whom Cochran brought over in *London, Paris, and New York* at the London Pavilion, 1921.

15. The original *Co-Optimists*, Royalty Theatre, 1921. Up and down the trellis: Laddie Cliff, Phyllis Monkman, Melville Gideon, Babs Valerie, Stanley Holloway, Davy Burnaby, Elsa Macfarlane, H. B. Hedley, Betty Chester, and Gilbert Childs.

16. The arrival of the unexpected daughter. After twenty years Blacky II (Mary Odette) proves her identity to her father, Lieutenant-Colonel Waverley Ango (Godfrey Tearle) in *The Faithful Heart*, Comedy Theatre, 1921.

17. *A Bill of Divorcement*, St. Martin's, 1921: Meggie Albanesi interrupts a scene between her father and mother (Lilian Braithwaite and C. Aubrey Smith).

18. The "old bolter" tells Elizabeth not to follow her example: Lottie Venne and Fay Compton in Somerset Maugham's *The Circle* at the Haymarket, 1921.

19. Gladys Cooper in *The Sign on the Door*, Playhouse, 1921: "I killed him! He attacked me, and I killed him!"

20. Edna Best, in *Polly With a Past* (St. James's, 1921), wore a Reville model "embellished with wreaths of flowers in orange, yellow, and cerise", and "a head-dress of birds-of-paradise".

21. "Stap me vitals!": Charles Hawtrey "applejacking" during the dream scene of *Ambrose Applejohn's Adventure* at the Playhouse, 1921.

22. Sally in the Ballet: Dorothy Dickson, in *Sally* (Winter Garden Theatre, 1921), "takes the leading part in the Butterfly Ballet and has no more dishes to wash. Henceforward all goes well with her, and," wrote a rapturous critic, "she ends her wonderful career by marrying the man she loves who happens to be a millionaire."

23. *The Sleeping Princess* at the Alhambra Theatre, 1921. The Wedding scene in Diaghilev's revival of the Tschaikowsky-Petipa ballet.

Not a major year; but it did leave with us two of the major plays of their period: W. Somerset Maugham's *The Circle* and Clemence Dane's *A Bill of Divorcement*. Astonishingly, *The Circle* was booed on the March night of its première at the Haymarket. The gallery could not always hear ("Don't mumble!" it shouted), and it did not like Maugham's irony. For all that, the play lasted through 180 performances, and New York agreed with the long-term verdict. In *The Circle*, Elizabeth, wife of a tediously priggish M.P., is tempted to escape with a young man from a rubber estate in Malaya. Her mother-in-law, Lady Kitty, who had eloped thirty years earlier with a young peer, has just come back to England from "a filthy marble palace in Italy". At the end, in spite of Elizabeth's father-in-law, a self-styled "downy old bird" who ponders epigrams in a cottage on the estate, there is indeed another elopement, and the circle is completed: not before Maugham has kept the piece moving on its plane of high comedy through three expertly-ordered acts, composed with a precise, needled wit. The gallery could not have realised in that noisy March that, thirty years on, the critic of *The Times* would be saying: "It is hard to believe that a comedy which, from end to end, gives the effect of sparkle and wit without detracting from its own truth will not outlast many theatrical fashions."

On the first night of *The Circle* Fay Compton—straight from her long run in *Mary Rose*—had a telegram from Gerald du Maurier that said urgently: "Don't disappear in this play. I couldn't bear it." He would not have minded the disappearance Maugham arranged for her at the last, with Lottie Venne, Allan Aynesworth, and Holman Clark left on the stage "in fits of laughter" not entirely unanimous. Ernest Thesiger, who had been the gillie in *Mary Rose* and who now made a poker-work masterpiece of the pompous husband, found the part complex at first: he says that, at one moment, he and the producer being at variance and the author being out of the country, he "nearly sent an expensive cable to China to ask Maugham what he meant my character to be feeling in one important scene".

Maugham was already nearly two-thirds of the way through his career as a dramatist. In *A Bill of Divorcement* Clemence Dane (pseudonym of Winifred Ashton, herself an actress) was beginning hers, and beginning it finely. Her play, extremely contentious in its time, can scorch a theatre years after the reform it called for (that lunacy should be a just ground for divorce) has been conceded. It was itself set in a conjectural future. Recommendations of the "Majority Report of the Royal Commission on Divorce" had become law, and under them a woman had divorced her husband—a war shell-shock victim—who had been for sixteen years in an asylum. A week before she hoped to marry again, her husband, sanity restored, escaped and returned to his home.

Here was a grimly dramatic situation in the theatre. Lilian Braithwaite and Malcolm Keen knew how to hold it, and Meggie Albanesi, as the daughter of the house, kept the reputation that she had already won at the St. Martin's. Finally, the wife went with her lover; father and daughter remained together. Most reasonably, the play ran and ran. By then the St. Martin's, under the Reandean management, had become the connoisseurs' corner of the West End. Playgoers who saw *A Bill of Divorcement* there, and who expected Miss Dane to keep to the same track, were startled—not too strong a word—to find what her next play would be.

Towards the end of 1921 her name appeared on the Shaftesbury Theatre programme of *Will Shakespeare*, a full-scale verse drama at a time when there were very few. It is usual for historians to ignore *Will Shakespeare*, and to go to Flecker's *Hassan* as the first verse play in the West End theatre after a long gap. They ought not to under-value Miss Dane's drama. It has plenty of fervour, some hot, bold verse, and one of the most plausible stage portraits of Elizabeth, who has frequently been just a Tudor in a tantrum behaving like Alice's Red Queen. Miss Dane had no kind of fortune. It seemed that even the cautious label of "an invention" could not excuse a plot in which Shakespeare surprised Christopher Marlowe at a Deptford assignation with Mary Fitton (the Dark Lady), and, accidentally, stabbed him to death.

Before the production the players had gone down to Stratford-upon-Avon to be photographed. They acted away dutifully in the Birthplace, upon Clopton Bridge, and on that highly uncomfortably settle in the Hathaway cottage; but the visit was not the luck-bringer it ought to have been. London took the piece sluggishly. Records show that Philip Merivale looked like Shakespeare, and that Haidée Wright acted Elizabeth with her special quality of imaginative possession. No matter. A young playgoer who combs the programme to-day, will not look twice at the principals. Instead, he will probably snatch from the list of walkers-on the name of Flora Robson, just as, in looking at the first Haymarket programme of *The Circle*, he will notice

Cecil Trouncer as the footman. In 1944, on the same stage, Trouncer would
be Arnold Champion-Cheney, the husband.

    Will Shakespeare was one of the losses of the year of failure. So, too, if
we depend on statistics, was *Heartbreak House*, at the Court Theatre in Sloane
Square, Bernard Shaw's first major work for some years, and one that though
it did not take the stage until 1921 had been written at intervals between
1913 and 1919. The "fantasia in the Russian manner on English themes"
is a summary of Shavian thought and experience: a satirical comment upon
the heartbreak house that was cultured, leisured pre-war Europe, and the
leisured class that had let civilisation slip into bankruptcy. Some of it is
perverse, some incandescent. Certainly it defeated its first audience and the
critics. Arnold Bennett went to sleep twice. Next morning the newspapers
talked of "Scatterbrain House" and "Jawbreak House", and nobody knew
what to make of Shotover, railing Isaiah, crazy sea-captain, whose scenes
with the girl Ellie Dunn are Shaw's nearest approach to poetry. Time has
burnished the play. Now, when critics quote, they go to Shotover's warning
against a blind trust in providence, and his answer to Hector who has asked
what an Englishman's task might be: "Navigation. Learn it and live; or
leave it, and be damned."

    Another so-called failure, and one that has not survived here as *Heart-
break House* has done—indeed it faded like a wisp of cirrus into the autumn
night—was Sacha Guitry's *Deburau*. It came to the Ambassadors Theatre in
a version by Harley Granville-Barker that mixed prose, blank verse, and
rhyme. According to the play, Jean Gaspard Deburau, great Parisian mime
of the eighteen-forties, loved unavailingly the *cocotte* Marie Duplessis, and
found for her the name by which she would always be called:

> My lady with the camellias.
>   Why?
> Because I shall always see you
> As first I saw you stand
> With the flickering light upon you
> And that flower in your hand.

Robert Loraine, if not the most wistful of actors, was an eloquent Deburau;
but there was a general feeling that the play did not come off, which meant

that, presently, after twenty-eight performances, it did. In *Deburau* the young composer Ivor Novello had his first brief acting part, "A Young Man".

During the month of November, while *Deburau* was failing, a greater failure saddened theatrical London, that of the full-length classical ballet of *The Sleeping Princess* in Diaghilev's season at the Alhambra. For students this was a glittering adventure. Spessivtseva (Spessiva), Trefilova, and Egorova were the three Princesses; later Lopokova and Nemchinova appeared. The production ran for 105 performances, which may not seem to us now like failure; but as Dame Ninette de Valois, looking back, has said, though Diaghilev's small coterie of followers for his modern works would support him handsomely for a six-week season, London did not have the public for a three-month season of one classical ballet of such dimensions as *The Sleeping Princess*. It was very costly, with its sets by Bakst and its hundred costumes, and the expensive venture came to a dolorous end when, after a quarrel between the backer (Sir Oswald Stoll) and Diaghilev, costumes and scenery were placed in store from which, years later, they emerged almost ruined by damp. Lopokova, in a curtain speech on the last night at the Alhambra, said gallantly that the company would soon be coming back, "very good-humoured ladies". Not so; three years passed before London saw the Ballet again. This may be difficult to credit now; but it was 1921, the sun had not begun to rise over Sadler's Wells or Covent Garden, and not many people had learned the language of ballet. It would be a long time yet before Hermione Baddeley, in revue, would dance Madame Allova to Cyril Ritchard's Harold Helpmeet in *The Creaking Princess*. That was in another decade, another age, and—I regret—outside this book.

The playgoer of 1921 had his gaieties. If he went to Wyndham's—and he would have been a very odd playgoer if he did not—he would have seen Gerald du Maurier (knighted early in 1922) shattering the plans of Peterson and Lakington, breaking up a bogus nursing-home, rough-housing in the laboratory, throttling the doctor, and making it clear that "thick-ear play" meant what it said. Du Maurier flicked off the phrase in a speech on the triumphant first night.

Collectors of the first-night scene had a good year. Probably the gayest moment of all came at the end of *Christopher Sly* when, after Matheson Lang had spoken a soliloquy twenty-five minutes in length, the Italian dramatist Forzano took a call, flung his arms round Lang, and kissed him passionately on both cheeks. Nothing like that happened at the première of Walter Hackett's *Ambrose Applejohn's Adventure*—so much better a title than the original *Spanish Treasure*—but it was some time before the audience was coaxed out of the Criterion. This was the farce in which Charles Hawtrey's Applejohn, dreaming while crooks ransacked his Cornish mansion, appeared in the second act as his ancestor, Applejack the pirate, crying "Scum!" and "Blast ye!", terrorising the mutineers, and observing of a sudden that he was in "a mood for dalliance". Funny in any circumstances, it became all the funnier when it was Hawtrey, silkiest of contemporary comedians, that thundered suddenly beneath the folds of the Jolly Roger.

For him *Applejohn* was a blessed relief after the boredom of an earlier part in *Up in Mabel's Room*, a cheap little comedy that quivered about like a crane-fly. Everything rested on a missing chemise, a word that the Lord Chamberlain would not allow to be spoken. Instead everyone called it "Mabel's whereabout" or "that little piece of evidence". Hawtrey spent most of the evening under Mabel's bed, and playgoers were duly shocked.

Not much else shocked them during the year. They took serenely the blinding of Sybil Thorndike in *The Old Women*, and the other excesses of Grand Guignol. They did not mind hacked-up versions of best-selling novels by Gertrude Page and Ethel M. Dell. And they applauded two dramas in which Godfrey Tearle appeared, Monckton Hoffe's agreeably sentimental anecdote of *The Faithful Heart* with twenty years between the acts, and Mary Odette to double mother and daughter, and Channing Pollock's vigorous American invention, *The Sign on the Door*, with Gladys Cooper ("I killed him! He attacked me, and I killed him!") in the fell clutch of circumstance. Tearle also acted Othello in a rather better play than either of the others, but less agreeable to the public. Shakespeare just then was not sovereign with Londoners, in spite of Lilian Baylis's endurance at the Old Vic, and J. B. Fagan's less sustained efforts at the Court where Tearle played Othello.

Not very much of worth had yet arrived from America: merely, as I have put it elsewhere, a few Belasco dramas, a barrel or so of molasses, and various bedroom capers of the kind that, with musical "swarries" and spy melodramas, composed so much of the war-time theatre of amusement. Plays often took a few years to cross the Atlantic. Thus an American farce, *Polly With a Past*, that had a moderate success at the St. James's in 1921, had been done on Broadway in 1917. There seemed to be no valid reason for reviving

it. Possibly one playgoer in fifty thousand has heard of the piece to-day,
or can say who Polly was, or what was her past. I call it up now because
the London company included Edna Best, Donald Calthrop, C. Aubrey
Smith, Edith Evans, Helen Haye, Henry Kendall, Claude Rains, and the
young man, Noël Coward, who had written "I'll Leave It To You." His part in
Polly bored him; but he amused himself, outside the theatre, by writing much
at high speed (including a comedy, *The Young Idea*), and, within the theatre,
by "embroidering and overacting" his minor part to such an extent that
Donald Calthrop and Henry Kendall "had to fight like steers to get their
lines over at all".

Dramatists had to fight like steers to get their plays over. Lord Dunsany
had a gentle success with *If*, based on the tiny incident that can change a
life. What would have happened on a given day, ten years before, if a
respected City man had caught the 8.15 instead of missing it? When this
John Beal (Henry Ainley played him) went back to the past, with the aid
of a useful Oriental talisman, he duly missed the train and became presently
a harassed despot in a place "off the map", but near Persia. A. A. Milne
wrote a play of heavier metal than usual, *The Truth About Blayds*, which was
put on just before Christmas and had one of the best first acts of the Twenties.
In this we met the secretively senile poet Blayds (Norman McKinnel, with his
expressive eye-work), who was not entitled to the poems that had made his
name. It was a richly theatrical idea that Milne could not develop, but the
play was far from a failure.

Perhaps the most blazing failure of 1921 was a biography of Byron,
The Pilgrim of Eternity, in which eternity dwindled to nine performances—in
spite of the presence of Yvonne Arnaud as the Countess Guiccioli. Byron in
the theatre has been as luckless as peacocks' feathers or the *Macbeth* music.
This particular failure was staged at the Duke of York's which, like so many
London theatres then, had no policy but took anything that was going.
Few theatres, in fact, were left, except those devoted to musical comedy, at
which a playgoer knew exactly the sort of entertainment he would get. Thus
the Duke of York's programme during the year covered *Lonely Lady*, *Mis'
Nell of New Orleans*, *The Tartan Peril*, *The Wrong Number*, and *Charley's Aunt*.

Just as haphazard was the Princes Theatre list: Sarah Bernhardt season,
Russian Ballet, *The Knave of Diamonds*, D'Oyly Carte Opera Company in
Gilbert and Sullivan. The Lyceum, after a "romance of the West", *The*

Savage and the Woman, put on revivals of *Abraham Lincoln* and *The Only Way*; *Cinderella* looked in at Christmas, more certain of her welcome than any of the others had been. To thicken the confusion, these were days of wild criss-cross transferences. A fairly good comedy might flit to three theatres within a few weeks. It looked well on the touring posters: "The great success from the Royalty, Apollo, and St. James's Theatres, London."

One or two theatres kept a policy. You could always count on du Maurier at Wyndham's, and, generally, on Lang at the New. But the high days of actor-management were all but over. Occasionally the stage seemed to be at some eccentric round of musical chairs or general post. It was gay enough, for this was still at the beginning of the long interval. "Years and years of afternoon" lay ahead. The light musical theatres were the most consistent, though some (the Gaiety for one) could search in desperation for the right play. Hence the Gaiety's awed flirtation with Maeterlinck's fairy play, *The Betrothal* (Gladys Cooper as Joy), and the appalling collapse of an effort to relight what was called, sentimentally, the Sacred Lamp of Burlesque, with something entitled *Faust-on-Toast*: part-author, Firth Shephard; Jack Buchanan as Faust; Maisie Gay as Martha. Two different versions put up thirty-four performances between them.

Daly's, the Winter Garden, and the Adelphi were safe for musical comedy of various types: lushly opulent and romantic at the first theatre, young and lively at the second, and, at the third, with a framework steady enough to support the generously broad nonsense of the house comedian, W. H. Berry. Cochran guarded the Pavilion; Charlot's revues ribboned out at the Vaudeville; there was usually hope at the Alhambra, the Oxford, and the Prince of Wales; and, while Oscar Asche ruled, there would be camels at His Majesty's. Now a new name had reached the West End stage: *The Co-Optimists.*

The concert-party so entitled—the first resolute experiment since Pélissier's Follies—put on an opening programme at the Royalty, freed suddenly by the death of *The Cinema Lady* after its sustained life of three performances. The next audience in the theatre, on the night of June 27, discovered that it was watching a pierrot-show ("Bow-wow!"), with the artists, in skull-caps, ruffles, and pom-poms, sitting round in a semi-circle, accompanied by a pair of pianos, and with no scenery except curtains and a couple of trellised columns joined by a garland. Davy Burnaby, solid and bland, led the company; the Royalty season went to 500 performances; and *The Co-Optimists*, in sundry programmes at sundry theatres, did not disband until 1927. They came together again for a short time in 1929, but their last appearance in 1935 fizzled gloomily in a theatre that had no time for the past.

During most of the Twenties the Co-Optimist purple and gold were the club colours of the most endearing of diversions. One of the names was Melville Gideon, the pianist, of whom James Agate would write one day: "With his crumpled, monkeyish mask, admirably assumed and hardly ever discarded, his unaffected ease, his crooning of sentimentalities in so low a voice that they reach what old-fashioned people still call the heart, his voluntary jazzing and guying of the same melodies so that they are purged of treacle, his knack of charming the tinniness out of a piano—all these qualities might entitle this artist to declare: *Le Co-Optimisme, c'est moi*." The company's secret was its friendliness. It expressed the amiable everyday humour of the Twenties, the gay froth of existence. The players established a pier-head in Central London, and they kept it until spontaneity had gone, and what had been at first fresh and buoyant, lapsed into tired routine.

In the year of *The Co-Optimists* London met the hardly comparable Théâtre de la Chauve-Souris. This was the Bat Theatre of Moscow, so named, it appeared, because its first home was a cellar from which a bat flew out at the opening of the door. Charles Cochran had seen the company in Paris, and, dazzled by its cabaret-vaudeville programme, hastened to bring it to the London Pavilion. It was not altogether the golden success he had imagined. One critic, calling it Cochran's master-stroke, hugged himself at the thought of the toy soldiers that swayed sideways and all but toppled over, and described Nikita Balieff, the compère, who resembled a great grey hawk, as a master of grimace "as much as Grimaldi, Grock, and Pélissier rolled into one". Another commented sourly: "Little more than a glorified cabaret series of short turns, not all of which are novel, artistic, or stimulating."

Balieff let it be understood that he knew very little English, but he appeared to talk it well enough in practice; certainly he knew just enough to realise what the effect of a very little could be. When he had lumbered before the curtain to point out that "the subject is very simple, but the music is more simple than the subject", everything had been said that could

25. Aided by a feather fan, Dorothy Dickson sings the fox-trot song, "Dancing Time," in *The Cabaret Girl* at the Winter Garden Theatre, 1922.

24. Beatrice Lillie sings "The Girls of the Old Brigade" in *The Nine O'clock Revue* at the Little Theatre, 1922.

26. The Trix Sisters, Helen and Josephine, in Jack Hylton's *The Cabaret Follies* on the Queen's Hall Roof, 1922.

27. Schober (Percy Heming), in *Lilac Time* at the Lyric Theatre, 1922: "Won't you stay, Miss Lili? We're just going to try over Franz's last song—the one dedicated to you. It is a great honour to have a song of Schubert's dedicated to you." Schubert was played by Courtice Pounds and Lili by Clara Butterworth.

28. Phyllis Dare, with fan and train, makes an entrance in *The Lady of the Rose* at Daly's Theatre, 1922.

29. Binnie Hale and Cyril Maude practising the "Eskimo Lumber" in Ben Travers's *The Dippers*, Criterion Theatre, 1922.

30. Mary Brough, Yvonne Arnaud, and Ralph Lynn, in *Tons of Money* (Shaftesbury Theatre, 1922), are waited on at breakfast by Ena Mason and George Barrett.

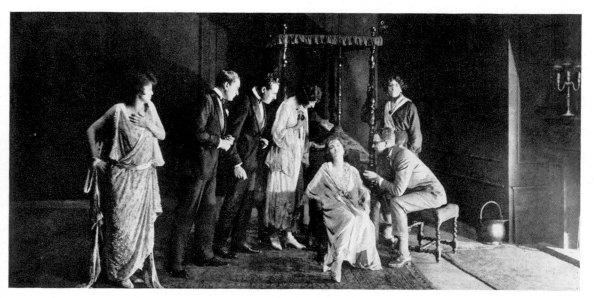

31. Annabelle (Mary Glynne) collapses in the bedroom of the clutching hand, and the house-party comes to her rescue. A scene from *The Cat and the Canary* (Shaftesbury Theatre, 1922), with Auriol Lee, Evan Thomas, S. J. Warmington, Sheila Courtenay, Frank Denton, and Esmé Beringer.

32. Edith Evans as Cynthia Dell in *The Laughing Lady* at the Globe Theatre, 1922. The play was by Sutro, the gown by Worth.

33. Marie Löhr, in *The Return* at the Globe Theatre, 1922, models Worth's "flowing draperies of snow-white chiffon."

34. *The Man In Dress Clothes* at the Garrick Theatre, 1922: Seymour Hicks in his own adaptation of the French comedy. It ran for 233 performances and had four London revivals.

be said. Noël Coward parodied him in the agreeable sentence: "There iss an old Russian proberb wheech say that a dead rhinosceros iss nearer to the starrs than a little child who steecks a pean eento iss old grandmother, all of wheech have no bearing whatever upon the leetle scene wheech my company weel present."

Applause appeared to have no bearing whatever upon the luck of the Chauve-Souris. During ten weeks at the Pavilion and the Apollo, Cochran lost money, though excited news of the company's genius, and tales of the Volga Boat Song, the Wooden Soldiers' parade, and the polychrome of Russian peasant costumes, brought to the Pavilion such people as Ellen Terry and Charlie Chaplin. Balieff, shrugging, had the last word: "Bacon—particularly with eggs—will always be more popular in England than Shakespeare." (Later, the Chauve-Souris would come back to London in triumph).

Earlier in the year Cochran, most idealistic of showmen, had lost £5,000 on the Russian Ballet at the Princes, a season that included the bewildering *Chout*. It was probably with some relief that he turned to another Pavilion revue—nothing Russian in it—in the vein no other impresario has ever approached. Always he would make his revues of the most diverse elements. Here he had such artists as the Italian clowns, the Fratellini (who were booed on the first night: Cochran had a luckless love of circus slapstick); Alfred Lester, who sang "Ours is a nice 'ouse, ours is"; and the young artists, Evelyn Laye and June. June, sticking to her single name, sang "Whose baby are you?" with Clifton Webb.

It was ironical that this Pavilion revue, *The Fun of the Fayre*, should have siphoned off the public from the other major Cochran production of the year, *The League of Notions*. That ran at the New Oxford Theatre (a Corner House now occupies the site), which had been handsomely re-designed, even its bar turned into a Louis XVI drawing-room. *The League*, and its curtain of silver tissue, will be remembered for the Dolly Sisters, Rosie and Jennie, from America, who might not have been major players, but who had tremendous vitality and good nature. They helped to keep going through its rehearsals a costly production subject to all the shocks that revue on this scale is heir to: Cochran would have nothing but the best, and any failure would be more than commonly expensive. "I had," he says, "bought silks from America which I could not find elsewhere; I had Batik work done in New York; I had searched Paris for other materials, and ultimately had to

c

get it made specially in Lyons. I had bought from America lamps for stage lighting which then could not be obtained in England."

Happily, all went well, but it was an indifferent year for the stage, a simmering-hot summer did not help, and at length one of Cochran's own productions proved to be too strong a rival. For some reason, perhaps loyalty, when Cochran followed *The League of Notions* by his only pantomime, *The Babes in the Wood*, he cast the Dollys as the strangest Babes that those much-tried robins had seen in the theatre. Even their song "Keep on humming" could not keep the pantomime humming for longer than a month. Children, for whom it was primarily designed, must have found it puzzling. The Dolly Sisters—so blissfully American—aside, the production was not so much every child's glass of ginger-beer as the exceptional child's cup of hot chocolate, served in the most delicate of Sèvres porcelain.

Meanwhile, London had plenty to choose from in other musical plays. At His Majesty's Oscar Asche, whom nothing on a small scale would ever content, had taken a familiar risk and tried to repeat a triumph. This time the musical melodrama was *Cairo*, successor to *Chu-Chin-Chow*. Originally it had been christened *Mecca*, a name that a jealous rival of Asche forced him to alter on the plea that it would give offence, and the plot did not derive, as *Chu* had done, from the Arabian Nights. Asche, who wrote the book and lyrics, "a mosaic in music and mime", to music by Percy Fletcher, considered it to be "the heaviest and most elaborate production ever put upon the English stage". Undeniably a substantial and pictorial pageant, it survives in record for one scene only, a Bacchanalian orgy in a ruined palace "where, perchance, Cleopatra and her countless lovers, ages ago, did carouse, disport and sin". This was followed at once by a scene, on the edge of daybreak, in which several hundred dancers had collapsed, exhausted, on floor and staircase, "a human débris" (according to Archibald Haddon, the drama critic) "massed, conglomerate, their white limbs gleaming in the moonlight and the torches' glow . . . The festival of Saturn in ancient Rome could not have been more ravishing to the eye." Praise indeed from Haddon who had not always been a Cochran man.

Another critic, intending to be rude, likened the scene to "a shoal of mackerel cast up on a beach in moonlight—and almost as beautiful". Rightly, Asche pounced: "I have seen a haul of mackerel drawn ashore, but never in moonlight—and a most beautiful sight it was. Moonlight would add to it." Anyway, this particular orgy ran briskly at His Majesty's for nine months, and, in spite of sour-grape rumours, made a profit of £12,000. "I should like to have a lot of financial failures like that," put in Asche.

Elsewhere, the musical-comedy world beyond the moon was much as usual. Playgoers had not yet surrendered to the dance. A time would come when any musical comedy must be danced through at speed, every heel spilling gunpowder. But in 1921 they liked their plays to be either as sturdily romantic as *Sybil*, at Daly's, with Cossacks and Grand Dukes and José Collins; or as preposterous as *The Golden Moth*, at the Adelphi, which was founded on the Macaire-Strop legend—what Irving would have said we can merely guess—and had a book by P. G. Wodehouse and music by Ivor Novello. For the romantics Thorpe Bates sang inimitably "Dear eyes that shine", and for the others there was W. H. Berry, who for twenty years had been at only two theatres, Daly's and the Adelphi, and who here sang "Dartmoor Days":

> Just a happy band of sinners
>   Picking oakum and the winners
> In that dear, old-fashioned prison of mine.

W. H. Berry, with his popping eyes, was a dear old-fashioned comedian. He worked very hard and self-consciously (he had a habit of adding "Ahem!" to every written joke, and he did much the same in the theatre). But he could assume dignity that was broadly comic; he could bang over a song as well as any comedian of his era; and although he used innumerable properties, he could claim at least that he used them inventively.

Up in Leicester Square that spring, *The Rebel Maid*—in which Thorpe Bates sang before going on to *The Golden Moth*—arrived at the Empire with a libretto that could cover William of Orange and Septimus Bunkle. Better, it had a lusty baritone ballad called "The Fishermen of England", that would be heard later from nearly every amateur operatic stage. Just before the year went out, *Sally* came in at the Winter Garden, with Jerome Kern's music and Dorothy Dickson. Before this she had been a dancer only, with her husband, Carl Hyson, but it was clear that she could be equal to any musical-comedy heroine. She soon resolved the doubts of her composer who could not forget that Marilyn Miller had played his Cinderella-kitchenmaid in New

York. One of the echoes from the Gay Twenties is Dorothy Dickson's voice in "I'm just a wild, wild rose". Some may also remember, with a mild shudder, the Butterfly Ballet, its hollyhocks and trellis and its alarming lepidoptera.

We can leave the year 1921 to the sound of another famous voice of the decade, Beatrice Lillie. On Christmas Eve she appeared at the Vaudeville in André Charlot's revue, *Pot Luck* (written by Dion Titheradge and Ronald Jeans), which ran on well into the summer of 1922. Beatrice Lillie has been herself alone since she went on the stage; she owes nothing to anybody. The slim woman with the boyish, sleek hair, the quiver at the corners of the mouth and the needle in the eye, has a genius for what seems to be im-provisation. Her work is considered to the twitch of an eyelash, but she makes it appear spur-of-the-moment. Shoddy material is decorated until it gleams. A flick of the voice is a brushful of goldleaf. All the while she is whispering: "Both of us know this is rather absurd. Just pretend for a moment it's rather good." It is more; it can be miraculous, especially when she is preparing joyfully to puncture any irrelevant bit of drama.

Behind the fooling is a calm, laughing intelligence; in Beatrice Lillie's presence the brash or the cocksure must wilt. In her eye is a glint of disdainful mischief. When we see it, a phrase for another Beatrice shines in the mind, "What, my dear Lady Disdain!" and, with this, Beatrice's own confession, "I was born to speak all mirth and no matter." Undoubtedly, after *Pot Luck*, as so often since then, playgoers came a trifle dazed, into the Strand, remembering the trembling of an eyelash, but not a word anybody else had spoken all night.

IV

1922

So forward to 1922, the year—theatrically—of music and melodrama on which Beatrice Lillie would assuredly turn a bland and mocking eye. She did so in *The Nine o'Clock Revue* at the Little: no one has looked more unnaturally demure than that Girl of the Old Brigade. This was the first harvest-year of the mechanical shockers: not the Grand Guignol's ventures into the macabre—mocking Fate arranged that Beatrice Lillie should follow them on the Little Theatre stage—but the kind of murder play that now, in retrospect, must remind me of Robin Oakapple's suggestion to Old Adam Goodheart, "How would it be, do you think, were I . . . by making hideous faces at him, to curdle the heart-blood in his arteries, and freeze the very marrow in his bones?" To which Old Adam replies sourly: "It would be simply rude—nothing more."

Still, dramatists, and especially American dramatists, were resolved to try. For the most relentless, as I have said before, any evening had to be tied into an ensanguined knot, with all hands crowding to the panel. Never were faces more hideous. Walls opened, doors flew back, masked figures appeared, bookcases moved. There were shots in the dark, screams in the twilight, cats among the pigeons, and bats in the belfry. Rightly, one of the first American shockers—and I do not forget such earlier work as *The Thirteenth Chair* during the war—was called *The Bat*: Mary Roberts Rinehart and Avery Hopwood wrote it. John Willard wrote the other frenzied classic, *The Cat and the Canary*. Each had the midnight scurry, the masked figure in a gloom bitumen-black, the sudden powdery phosphorescence, the scrawny hand groping round the wall ("An Inexplicable Horror"), the comic maid-servant for relief who quavered into hysterics, the fixing of suspicion on each member of the cast in turn.

Such plays as these came to be known as thrillers: a horrible coinage, debasing a fine old Elizabethan verb. It ruins for us such lines as Juliet's

"I have a faint cold fear thrills through my veins that almost freezes up the breath of life." In *The Cat and the Canary* John Willard assumed from the first that none would be remotely surprised by a call to a midnight will-reading in a lonely house beside the Hudson River. This is quite a normal practice: no will can have a useful First Reading in any other circumstances. (One takes for granted the presence of a West Indian Negress babbling of evil spirits.) Moreover, if the will insists that the beneficiary shall spend the night in the bed where the testator died, who can reasonably grumble? If it is twenty years, to the hour, since the testator's death, that makes it all the more normal.

To-day, were *The Cat and the Canary* revived—and indeed it has been done at some of Britain's more catholic repertory theatres—we might be glad, sentimentally, to see the familiar Library and Bedroom again. Newcomers are bound to be less impressionable: juveniles fresh to the once famous jingle, "If you like this play, please tell your friends, but pray don't tell them how it ends." Today's cats, whether on hot tin roofs or not, do not belong to Mr. Willard's nether-world; but this play, in remembrance, rings a tinny bell in the caverns of the mind, even if it has long ceased to freeze up the breath of life.

The *Cat* rested upon an attempt to beat down a girl's sanity. As for *The Bat*, absolutely nothing to do with the one that whisked from the Chauve-Souris cellar, this was among the first of the plays in which detective turned out to be criminal: it could have entered James Agate's crowded category of the All-Along Drama. The authors botched their work by allowing a farcically frightened maidservant to rip open the suspense whenever possible. Even with this bawling, with the steeping of the stage in a sickly green, and with a failure to make any of the action mildly credible, *The Bat* managed to flap to success with a public that liked to be told a story, and did not much mind how improbable it was. There will always be this kind of audience: it can be maddening, but it can also disarm, and the most superior persons find themselves joining in the fun. Many more terrors would follow, as fast as dramatists could invent them and directors direct. Still, *The Bat* and the *Cat*, by themselves, would have made 1922 into an exceptional year. Eva Moore, as the sagacious Miss Van Gorder in *The Bat*, had her first "white-haired" part. She was also playing in a film called *Flames of Passion*: it was quite a year for her as well.

Otherwise, it was a year of marking time—for most people, that is, except Sybil Thorndike who, freed from Grand Guignol and with her eyesight safe, gave herself to Beatrice (in *The Cenci*), Medea, and Jane Clegg: a trinity one actress alone could manage. Fay Compton and Leon Quartermaine had an exhaustive and exhausting prowl through the generations in *Secrets*, by May Edginton and Rudolf Besier, a brand of melodramatic *Milestones* but extremely popular. Drury Lane, which had been reconstructed at a cost of more than £200,000, during the twelve months before April 1922, reopened with the garish spectacle of *Decameron Nights*, after Boccaccio: it cost another £40,000. There were forty-five speaking parts, with the Royal Hanging Gardens of Damascus, the vast terraced Palace of the Soldan, the Piazza di San Marco at Venice, and an eclipse of the sun. ("Showy, very showy—but isn't it a bit dull?" said somebody in James Agate's hearing.) It did not really quicken the pulse when Margaret Bannerman, who followed Wilette Kershaw as the heroine, was washed up, nude, on the shore, and borne off to safety by an aged monk in the faintest glimmer of steel-blue limelight.

Elsewhere, playgoers could wander between Maugham's *East of Suez*, on the Eurasian problem—it proved to be a scenario for a spectacular drama, with an early flourish of atmospherics in a Peking street—and the Dorset fishing village of Edward Percy's *If Four Walls Told*, with its hoary chimney-corner ancient as the life and heart of a tragi-comic plot. The play had some truth and savour besides its melodramatic lunge.

John Galsworthy this year came back to his most redoubtable form with *Loyalties*, a piece of social realism that considered caste warfare in Britain. It was forcibly argued, and it brought one uncanny performance from Ernest Milton as a young Jewish thruster, aflame with racial pride, who was in the right where snobbishness deemed that he should be in the wrong. In those days Milton, who had been acting at the Old Vic, could incinerate the theatre with a glance: mannerisms had not grown upon him, and few actors could so govern a stage upon entrance, or say so much without uttering a word. (A few years later Peter Godfrey would play this part with comparable intelligence at a provincial repertory theatre.)

Loyalties shared the St. Martin's bill with *Shall We Join the Ladies?*, a one-act puzzle that appeared for a single special performance in 1921, and that can continue to tantalise and to exasperate. It exasperates because it is the first act of a play that has not been completed—simply because (says Barrie's biographer, Denis Mackail) the dramatist could not finish it. "Nobody really minded who the murderer was, and if the author had been quite certain himself, and had gone on to tell them, it might easily have been a much flatter affair." A revival in 1950 showed it to be as sharp as ever it was, once we had resigned ourselves to the fact that nothing whatever would be explained, and that, from the first, Barrie—in his own vein of make-believe—had us neatly on toast, caring not for one moment who killed Cock Robin, or why. It is a masterly first act: a round-table conference that merely takes us round the table and back again. What might have happened if the authors of *Bat* or *Cat* had got their hands upon it, it is appalling to speculate.

The year had two depressing failures: one all the more depressing because a famous man of the theatre had failed with a theme meant for Barrie. The public could not have been more surprised if Barrie had written *The Notorious Mrs. Ebbsmith*. In this play, a "fable", *The Enchanted Cottage*, Sir Arthur Pinero tried to show how, through love, beauty is born. A young, war-broken man and an unattractive woman, who had married only as a formal gesture, "for mutual consolation", found true love under the spell of an enchanted cottage. Though all people except a blind man saw them as they were, Oliver and Laura would keep "fair and bonny" to each other while their love was constant. Alas, though Owen Nares and Laura Cowie acted with a glowing sincerity, refusing to bluff it through, the play never came alive in the theatre. After sixty-four performances it left the Duke of York's—a grief to anyone bred to the earlier work of Pinero, and not inclined to underrate what he had done for the stage.

At his height Pinero had absolute technical command: in *His House In Order*, for example. I suppose his name must always march with what Belloc's rhyme called "that interesting play, *The Second Mrs. Tanqueray*". It was some consolation to him that, in the summer and autumn of 1922, *Tanqueray* ("I believe the future is only the past again, entered through another gate") had a revival of five or six months at the Playhouse, acted with dignity and a certain precision and emphasis which even in the Twenties were passing from the theatre. Gladys Cooper got nearer to Paula than most people had hoped. No one has faulted the technique of *Tanqueray* except to mark those two clumsinesses in the first act, Aubrey's "Let me scribble a couple of notes now while I think of them" and "Perhaps you'll let me finish a couple of letters". There is, too, an unlucky passage later, Ardale's "Isn't

35. In *R.U.R.* (St. Martin's Theatre, 1923), Leslie Banks, as one of Rossum's Universal Robots, resists the humanising endeavours of Frances Carson.

36. John Gielgud as Felix, the butterfly, in the first scene of Čapek's fantasy, *The Insect Play*, at the Regent Theatre, 1923.

37. Yasmin (Cathleen Nesbitt) at window: "At last—at last! The Procession of Protracted Death! I shall see it all!" Hassan (Henry Ainley) is forced to witness the torments of Rafi (Basil Gill) and Pervaneh (Laura Cowie) in James Elroy Flecker's play at His Majesty's Theatre, 1923.

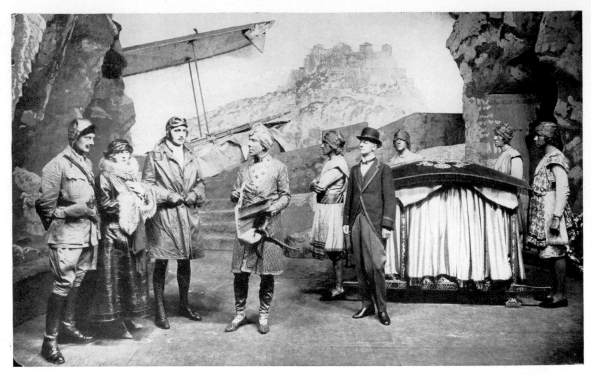

38. *The Green Goddess* (St. James's, 1923): The Raja of Rukh (George Arliss) greets the three visitors (Owen Roughwood, Isobel Elsom, George Relph) to his remote Himalayan kingdom: "You burned it to spare me a painful piece of intelligence. I already know what you tried to conceal: that three of my subjects have been sentenced to death."

39. Margot (Marie Löhr) and her repentant husband (Herbert Marshall) in Frederick Lonsdale's *Aren't We All?* at the Globe Theatre, 1923.

40. The masquerading Josephine (Peggy O'Neil) tries to dodge the latest story by her employer (John Deverell): a scene from *Plus Fours* at the Haymarket Theatre, 1923.

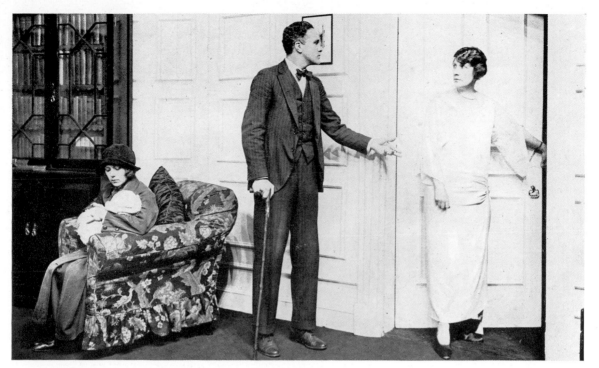

41. *If Winter Comes* (St. James's Theatre), 1923: Mrs. Sabre (Grace Lane): "You say this woman has a claim on us?" Mark (Owen Nares): Mabel, I do. I——" Mrs. Sabre: "Do you want my answer to that? My answer is that perhaps she has a claim on *you*!" The girl in distress is Effie (Helen Spencer).

42. Ann (Diana Hamilton) and Henry (William Stack) in *Outward Bound* (Garrick Theatre, 1923) are called back to life from attempted suicide. Scrubby is played by Stanley Lathbury.

43. "The dark star of the Plantation Revue," Florence Mills, in *Dover Street to Dixie* at the London Pavilion in 1923.

44. Fred and Adèle Astaire dance the Oom-pah Trot in *Stop Flirting* at the Shaftesbury Theatre, 1923.

45. "Other Girls": Noël Coward leads the chorus in one of his own numbers in *London Calling!* (Duke of York's Theatre, 1923), his first revue, written in association with Ronald Jeans.

this fun! A rabbit ran across my foot while I was hiding behind that old yew!" (Nobody has ever responded hilariously to that bit of off-stage fun.) These things aside, the woman with the past can still look to her theatrical future. Everyone regretted that by the Twenties Pinero had reached the evening of his powers. There would be one more play in the theatre, but that would not arrive until 1932: *A Cold June* indeed.

The other failure, besides *The Enchanted Cottage*, was Joseph Conrad's *The Secret Agent*. It lasted for only eleven performances at the Ambassadors: a shock to its acutely sensitive author who, like Henry James, had wished to conquer the stage. Much was written about *The Secret Agent*. J. T. Grein thought that the story of the anarchist, his avenging wife, and her trapped deceiver, might have prospered if it had been told directly. Conrad lacked two vital gifts: distribution and economy. Grein felt that he wanted a craftsman by his side to teach him the difference between stage and book, and to adapt both vision and expression to the peculiar focus of the theatre. W. A. Darlington put it succinctly: "When you came down to plain facts, what was wrong was that Conrad had joined Tennyson, Browning, and Stephen Phillips in Mr. Montague's category of writers who have not conformed to the conditions imposed by a particular kind of writing." Frank Swinnerton affirmed that the play had held him and moved him as no other had done in years. "The reason for the failure of *The Secret Agent* is that it made pleasure-loving audiences uncomfortable."

Pleasure-loving audiences had much with which to comfort themselves. They were not in the least worried at *Bluebeard's Eighth Wife*, a version from the French in which Hugh Wakefield had one of the few really comic drunk scenes, something roughed off as a rule in a sloppy stagger. They enjoyed the far quieter fun of *The Dover Road* (no rabbits or old yews), with Henry Ainley's overwhelmingly bland and leonine Latimer: Ainley could never help being leonine. Latimer made it his business to detain eloping couples for a while—he had his own methods—in the hope of discovering a change of heart. Invariably, the rest-cure worked. The play was Milne's variation on the "second chance" theme of Barrie's *Dear Brutus*.

In Alfred Sutro's well-carpentered comedy, *The Laughing Lady*, Edith Evans, in a small and "viperine" part, spoke in venomous italics. Ever a connoisseur's actress, the public was beginning to recognise her. *The Man in Dress Clothes* had Seymour Hicks (who took it from the French and acted

in it) as his usual bubble of mercury. Later a sentimental tremolo discon-
certed, but the play was boomed benevolently and unexpectedly by Lord
Northcliffe. Yet another Ethel M. Dell version ran for a while, this time
The Way of an Eagle, with her strong man dumber than ever. *Treasure Island*,
for which J. B. Fagan supplied most of the dialogue himself, a cunning pastiche,
also arrived this year, with Arthur Bourchier's Long John Silver in sleek
flamboyance; and Bruce Bairnsfather, for the Lyceum, evolved a ramshackle
drama called *Old Bill, M.P.*, with Edmund Gwenn as Bill. Characters named
Captain Lord Presentdale and Lieutenant Cheerio, M.C., were signs that
dramatists remained afraid to take the war seriously.

None of these matters could discomfit a playgoer. Certainly few would
have been discomfited by the birth of Aldwych farce. "Aldwych" farce, to
annoy a wearied historian, began at the Shaftesbury. Its first dramatist
was not Ben Travers, though that great farce-man had his first play staged
during the year in the underground bandbox of the Criterion. The skein
is twisted. I can untangle it by explaining that Aldwych farce opens officially
with *Tons of Money*, a complicated manœuvre by the comedian Will Evans,
and the writer who called himself "Valentine" (Archibald Thomas Pechey).
Completed before the outbreak of war in 1914, and produced at the Shaftesbury on April 13, 1922, it went to the Aldwych on October 30, and did
not leave that theatre until the early spring of 1924. *Tons of Money* made
£100,000 for its promoters, yet it had almost to be levered upon the stage.

During the autumn of 1921 Will Evans had met J. Bannister Howard, the
theatrical manager, in Manchester. In the best "Consequences" manner,
Evans said: "I have a farce." Howard said: "Right! I'll read it." The
consequence should have been an immediate production (and the world,
wise after the event, would have agreed). It did not come out like this.
Howard (as the authors had done) found an excited lack of enthusiasm.
Frank Curzon sent a telegram: "Burn it, forget it." Sir Alfred Butt refused
it, and so did most of the managements in London to whom it had been as
familiar as Big Ben. Then Howard sent it to Leslie Henson, who was equally
unsure. He passed it on to his new partners, Tom Walls—known at that
period only as a musical comedian—and Reginald Highley, who had been
Robert Courtneidge's manager, suggesting that they returned it to Howard.
But Highley, reading the typescript on the way to Brighton, thought it wildly
funny and alarmed other passengers by choking with laughter throughout

the journey. Tom Walls confirmed. Eventually, after some trouble, enough money was raised for a syndicate. *Tons of Money* went into rehearsal, where Yvonne Arnaud caused alarm by tripping over the phrase "Official Receiver" and making it "Official Retriever" ("We kept it in all right," recorded Valentine); and, at length, the morning arrived when a Southport newspaper observed: "There is not material here for three acts, and if those who are responsible for the production desire to make money, they might use what they've got as a framework for musical comedy or revue." Other critics were kinder.

Tons of Money reached London on the Thursday evening before Good Friday, which meant that there would be more space for reviews on Saturday. Nobody thought the space would be needed; but by the end of the night all the things that happen to critics on these occasions had occurred. Sides cracked; ribs were sore, or burst; laughter went hoarse. By the time that Louise (Yvonne Arnaud) had announced her last "idea", Aubrey (Ralph Lynn) had finished gnawing his knuckles, the solicitor (Robertson Hare) had declared yet again that he came from the firm of Chesterman, Chesterman, *and* Chesterman, and the three men with close-cropped beards had been confused with each other in all possible combinations, the Shaftesbury audience had seen that here was one of the biggest farcical hits on the English stage for years. It would have been hard to say why. It was just that the right actors had met the right script in the right atmosphere. Nora Heald, the acute drama critic of the *Daily Mail*, wrote nearly a column about the farce and its origin. The *Mail* continued with news-stories daily for a week or so, by which time, with other papers following, *Tons of Money* had begun to release its shower of gold. Twenty-one months later, when the run ended, Mary Brough, the deaf aunt never without her knitting on the stage, told the authors that she had been able to knit fourteen jumpers for her friends.

Also in the spring of 1922 a better farce, *The Dippers*, by a novelist, Ben Travers, was having a shorter run at the Criterion. Travers, who had conceived it as a farce, wrote one draft, and then re-cast it as a novel. But he knew that it would have to come to the stage, and it did, though the dramatist had the usual agonies to endure before Hawtrey (whom he had hoped would act in it) produced it for him, with Cyril Maude and Binnie Hale in the leads—and a young actress, Hermione Gingold, as a "walk-on", the Old Woman. The plot was, roughly, about a "specialty" dancer at a county ball who had been let down by her partner. Swiftly, she persuaded a kind and susceptible stranger to fill the gap before he understood what it might mean. For his benefit, a new dance, the Eskimo Lumber, had to be created. And so on: uncommonly crisp nonsense, important now as the beginnings of a master cracksman of his period. We find in it a song, "Dusky Nipper," for Binnie Hale: she and Maude danced to its music by Ivor Novello.

I have said before of Ben Travers—and I agree with my younger self— that he understands better than anyone the Farce of Situation. Other men's vision may be limited, but in Sam Weller's phrase he can see through a flight of stairs and a deal door. He can visualise a farce as it will be in performance; he knows to a hair the effect this line or that will have. Travers is a Lord of Misrule, with a genius for lyric, crumble-top absurdity. Farce needs a cracking pace, a fuming third-act rally, and dialogue that, even if it snows down into whirling flakes of nonsense, never freezes into the cold glitter of epigram. In 1922 the Aldwych and Travers had not met. They would; and the Twenties would be all the gayer for it.

Tom Walls, who had never been much regarded as an actor, managed that year to do a useful "double", appearing in the last act of *Tons of Money*, and also, at the Lyric Theatre earlier in the evening, as a hat manufacturer in the musical farce, *Whirled into Happiness*, adapted by Harry Graham from a Viennese original, with music by Robert Stolz. The cast is worth printing as a typical musical-comedy list of the early Gay Twenties:

Albert Horridge (Hat Manufacturer).....................Tom Walls
Horace Wiggs (Hairdresser's Assistant)..............Derek Oldham
Duke of Dulchester.................................Hastings Lynn
Marquis of Brancaster...........................Reginald Palmer
Captain Montagu Lush..........................Lawrence Phillips
Antoine (coiffeur)................................Frank Atkinson
Matthew Platt (attendant at the Majestic Music Hall)....Billy Merson
Delphine de Lavallière (Music Hall Star)...............Mai Bacon
Lily Brown (a manicurist).........................Peggy Maurice
Mrs. Horridge..................................Frances Wetherall
Duchess of Dulchester..............................Gladys Hirst
Fairy..Elsie Judge
Florence (the Horridges' daughter).................Winnie Melville
   Guests, Playgoers, Programme Sellers, Attendants, Servants, etc.

The first act was set in the foyer of the Majestic Music Hall, the second in the garden of Horridge's villa at Crouch End, and the third in Antoine's hairdressing establishment. The plot, after taking three acts to make up its mind, proved, not unexpectedly, that love will find a way. The music, forgotten now, tinkled pleasantly through the night. And little Billy Merson, an alert vaudeville comedian who was never more than alert though he could bang off a music-hall song with the needed attack, was in knockabout attendance, with ginger wig.

Various other more promising musical plays came to the West End that year. W. H. Berry, in *The Island King* at the Adelphi, sang "Will-i-am of Nor-man-dee" and "Old King Cole", and said to the island soothsayer Maru, bathed in green limelight, "You look more like a vegetable *Maru* to me" (Ahem!); Phyllis Dare was in one of the plushier Daly's operettas, *The Lady of the Rose* (a Baron Sprotti-Sprotti also in the cast); and the Gaiety, now under Robert Evett who followed George Edwardes at Daly's, and who left when the stormy financier James White took over, responded with Oscar Straus's *The Last Waltz*: José Collins, and a "Baron Ipporth Makowitch". In *The Cabaret Girl*, a Winter Garden musical, with Jerome Kern's score and book and lyrics by P. G. Wodehouse and George Grossmith, who wrote them on an Atlantic crossing, Dorothy Dickson again fluttered through the night, with Heather Thatcher as a personage named Little Ada.

The Cabaret Girl was a name that would help to train London to an idea it was only just beginning to take. Cabaret was slow in reaching us from America and the Continent. Conservative diners, forgetting the Bohemian supper-rooms (Evans's and the rest) of the Victorians, grumbled that they did not want to be distracted from their food and drink. One gourmet proclaimed that to be bullied into unwilling laughter at table was as bad as to eat with Mark Twain propped up behind his plate. (No doubt he meant one of Mark Twain's books, but the sight, however interpreted, seemed unlikely.) Some other anxious artists felt that they could hardly be expected to concentrate in an atmosphere where they would dwindle to an unwanted background noise. Neither argument mattered very much. Cabaret, accepted, began slowly to develop through the dancing mid-Twenties, even if as late as 1924 it was still by no means a commonplace. A few exclusive night-clubs, such as Murray's (where the twenty-one-year-old Gertrude Lawrence was singing and dancing in 1920), were the first real homes of cabaret; but the Hotel Metropole, in Northumberland Avenue, was the most persistent pioneer.

In 1922, when Sir Francis Towle proposed a "supper entertainment", George Grossmith, J. A. E. Malone, and André Charlot, his advisers, discovered that it was much easier to put on an elaborate revue in a theatre than to cope with a small cabaret for which L.C.C. regulations permitted six artists only, and in evening dress, without scenery or properties. The rules were finally relaxed, after a variety of rebuffs and a good deal of agitated official dithering that would have prevented men less resolute from carrying on. When the authorities were gentler, the Metropole would realise how unobtrusively its entertainment, *The Midnight Follies*, had become part of London's night-life. In the drizzling autumn of 1922 (Gertrude Lawrence was the leading lady that Christmas) it was in its birth-pangs. At that time we might have discovered one of the new diversions at what people, in later years, would say was a madly improbable address: the Queen's Hall Roof. But there it was, and with that energetic band-leader Jack Hylton to control *The Cabaret Follies* and to introduce such an act as the singers Josephine and Helen Trix.

Charles B. Cochran, who hated to be known as "C.B." as much as Shaw objected to his "George", would come into cabaret before long. Not just yet. He was having a very poor time. At the New Oxford he lost £20,000 on *Mayfair and Montmartre*, with Delysia, who had to leave the cast because of throat trouble; a Boccaccio scene (it was a year for the Decameron); an Inca ballet, an eighteenth-century Versailles spectacle which Walkley of *The Times* said had a "bizarre, Aubrey Beardsleyish beauty", and Nellie Taylor, as Gainsborough's Blue Boy—just sold to America—singing an early Cole Porter song:

> I'm bluer and bluer,
> Because I'm saying goodbye to
> London town.

A Pavilion production, the French musical play, *Phi-Phi*, was set in and about private rooms in a Roman bath. Cochran himself thought it vulgar, and it had a moderate run without the benefit—or otherwise—of the Press. Cochran, angry with the response to *Mayfair and Montmartre*, excluded the critics. "Probably," he wrote later, "I did myself service. If they had said half what I thought about *Phi-Phi*, we might not have had the five months' run." This was also the year of *Battling Butler*, with Jack Buchanan, for whose special charm we have again to call on Daisy Ashford's Earl of Clincham: "A tall man, with very nice eyes of a twinkly nature, and curly hair." It was the year of the Gay-Bax-Austin-Playfair *Polly*; of *The Immortal Hour* at King's Cross, to which we shall return in 1923; of Beatrice Lillie governing *The Nine o'Clock Revue* at the Little Theatre in the Adelphi; of the entrancing, or terrifying, musical biography, *Lilac Time*, Schubert and butterscotch, which would set a fashion; and, inevitably, *The Co-Optimists*, going on and on, with Betty Chester to sing "Sea Fever" in a voice from the abyss, Gilbert Childs in a bull-ring as Carmen-two-seater, Laddie Cliff with "Coal-Black Mammy", and Phyllis Monkman in exuberant dance.

The Hippodrome posters carried what sounded like a golfing title: *Round In Fifty*, a revue quite forgotten when, thirty-five years on, London crowded to the film of *Round the World in Eighty Days*. Sax Rohmer, Julian Wylie and Lauri Wylie based their revue on the Verne romance, with the difference that here George Robey, as the son of Verne's Fogg, won a wager of his own that took him from the Gridiron Club in London, round the world and back again. A. E. Wilson, Robey's biographer, remembers how Robey observed to a temptress, "It is women like you that make men like me like women like you." Audiences of 1922 thought it remarkable to see film sequences of the approach of an Atlantic liner, and of a race along the Portsmouth road that enabled Robey to win his wager (according to custom) just in time. No one was surprised at that.

V

1923

No one should have been surprised at anything George Robey did. In his time he could rule an audience, "merriment tempered with dignity", in any part from Sir John Falstaff to the Mayor of Muckemdyke, or, simply, the Robey figure with the bushy eyebrows, the long, black, collarless coat, the little flat bowler, and the swishing whangee cane. During the Thirties Horace Horsnell would write (in a journal then notable for its drama criticism): "As Robey enters from the wings, his eyes command the house like the blazing headlights of a car rounding the corner of a night-dark road." That was in the autumn of Robey's career. He had never lost his power of grabbing an audience—a quality we mourn in a day miserably microphone-bound. In 1923 he was not yet in the middle fifties, and very much master of the drolls. As I say, nothing he did should have surprised; but even his loyal subjects were astonished when he appeared on January 27 at the Royal Opera House, Covent Garden, in something described shamelessly as a "jazzaganza". Its title underscored the general feeling. It was *You'd Be Surprised*, to which Robey would have added, infallibly, "I meantersay!"

Sir Oswald Stoll put on the revue which was of American origin, but had the most wildly mixed cast: Arabian acrobatic dancers, the Savoy Havana Band, Lydia Lopokova, Leonide Massine, Leon Woizikowsky, the young Ninette de Valois, who danced a black-faced piccaninny in an interpolated Darius Milhaud ballet, a huge corps-de-ballet, and, of course, Robey, who had next to nothing to do that mattered. There had been much angry and humourless comment on his "presumption" in appearing at Covent Garden. Ninette de Valois records how he routed possible gallery demonstrations as soon as he entered: "With his finger on his lips he tiptoed straight down to the footlights; the eyebrows were raised higher than ever, but quizzically asymmetrical in their mock-agitation. 'Hush, hush,' he announced. 'You mustn't laugh here.'" A. E. Wilson tells us of another Robeyesque rebuke: "I had

46. Lydia Sokolova and Leon Woizikowsky in the contemporary Cocteau-Milhaud ballet, *Le Train Bleu*, during a Diaghilev season at the London Coliseum, 1924.

47. Aphrodite and Hymen (Lubov Tchernicheva and Anton Dolin) reward fidelity in *The Faithful Shepherdess*, London Coliseum, 1924.

48. Anna Pavlova and Laurent Novikoff in the ballet, *Don Quixote*, first danced in 1924 during a season at the Royal Opera House, Covent Garden. Pavlova is Kitry, the innkeeper's daughter, and Novikoff is Basil, the barber.

49. Zélie (Isabel Jeans) fails in a last effort to recapture Pierre Boucheron (Ivor Novello) in *The Rat* (Prince of Wales's Theatre, 1924). Pierre: "They're not beautiful hands; they're animal's hands."

50. The blinded officer (Henry Kendall) learns the truth from Violet (Frances Carson) in *Havoc* at the Haymarket Theatre, 1924: "Then you've never loved me—not even that night when you——."

51. "Mammy-palaver" in "the hot, damp, exhausting climate" of the West Coast of Africa: "Tondeleyo most interestin'." Brian Aherne and Mary Clare in *White Cargo* (Playhouse, 1924).

52. The victory of the tiger-cat wife: Suzanne (Edith Evans) brings André (Arthur Wontner) to her feet once more in *Tiger Cats* at the Garrick Theatre, 1924.

53. Sybil Thorndike in the closing lines of the Epilogue, *Saint Joan* (New Theatre, 1924): "O God that madest this beautiful earth, when will it be ready to receive Thy saints?"

54. "It doesn't matter about death, but it matters terribly about life": Noël Coward (Nicky Lancaster) with his mother (Lilian Braithwaite) at the final curtain of *The Vortex* (Everyman, Hampstead, 1924).

55. Third time lucky: Samuel Sweetland finds a bride. He continued to do so for 1,329 performances in the Birmingham Repertory Company's production of *The Farmer's Wife* at the Royal Court Theatre, 1924.

56. The Pounds *"empanachées"*: Lorna and Toots Pounds, the Australian sisters, in the London Palladium's 1924 revue, *The Whirl of the World*.

57. Sonnie Hale and his "Chili Bom-Bom" (Hermione Baddeley) in *The Punch Bowl*, a revue at the Duke of York's Theatre, 1924.

58. Tiara, orchids, and pearls: June as Princess Stephanie, and Jack Buchanan as Anthony Prince in *Toni*, a musical comedy at the Shaftesbury Theatre, 1924.

hoped—I say, I had hoped that my peregrinations from the halls of raucous song and ill-clad Terpsichore to this temple of ancient and classic consonance would have synchronised with a general improvement in your demeanour. But alas! I fear such is not the case." The revue had a very short run, went over to the more suitable surroundings of the Alhambra, and there had three performances a day—without the ballet—until it flickered away to become an entry in the files.

This was one of the freaks of a year of surprise. Flecker's *Hassan* was staged at last; the comedienne, Marie Tempest, long absent, came back to London in a dire failure; Tallulah Bankhead flared suddenly; Sybil Thorndike decided to play Imogen in London, and the Birmingham Repertory did a *Cymbeline* in modern dress; the same theatre was the first to attempt Shaw's cycle, *Back to Methuselah*; London met Florence Mills, the Astaires, and the robots; William Archer, sternest of drama critics, offered the swooping melodrama of *The Green Goddess*; and *Outward Bound*, by Vane Sutton Vane, had one of the most imaginatively chilling passages of dialogue the decade would know.

Hassan first. James Elroy Flecker, poet of the sun, who had died of consumption at Davos Platz in Switzerland early in 1915, had walked his bridge of fire between the East and West. He was the voice of the four Damascus gates, of Baghdad's "dim-moon city of delight", of the golden journey to Samarkand, of the swan-peaks of Lebanon, of the flower-poised Aegean isles. Loving the East, he tried to express it in verse as sharply cut as the mid-day shadow upon marble. Unluckily, though he had given his concentrated affection to *Hassan*, an exercise in the romantic-macabre, an Arabian Night of Haroun's Caliphate, the piece suffered from the density of its texture, its Oriental arabesques. Unlike the poems, the play did not strike sharply: its blade was muffled. Still, the Twenties needed high words. Basil Dean, a faithful friend to the play, had long corresponded with Flecker about it during the poet's life ("Can we have *real camels* for the first scene?" Flecker had asked pathetically). Now Dean assembled a very fine cast and arranged for production at His Majesty's. It was part of the bargain that he should first direct George Grossmith in a revival of *The Gay Lord Quex* which soon fizzled.

A few months later, after Drinkwater's *Oliver Cromwell*, with Henry Ainley ("I have said a word for freedom"), had been a dignified failure, *Hassan* at last reached the stage. "As the day drew near," Basil Dean wrote later, "public anticipation rose like a fever." Henry Ainley as Hassan, music

D

by Delius, ballets by Fokine, a vast company, production in the most sumptuous manner, as Flecker would have wished: the elements of triumph seemed to be here, and yet the play—though it ran for eight months and had its passionate admirers—was not the work of genius all had expected. Ainley's Hassan, like the production, was not more than solid: his darkly shining voice was there, not the imagination that should have winged it. Flecker's spirit shone most clearly through the tones of Leon Quartermaine as Ishak the poet ("Thy dawn, O Master of the World, thy dawn; the hour the lilies open on the lawn"). It was a pity, perhaps, that the theatre had to be His Majesty's. Memories of *Chu-Chin-Chow* and *Cairo* still tingled, and to put *Hassan* with these was a tempting piece of facile rudeness; detractors grasped it with delight.

The play had its passages of extreme beauty: its Prologue and Epilogue, each written first as a detached poem; the ghazel ("How splendid in the morning glows the lily!"), and several of the glittering speeches for Ishak. Other scenes, such as the poetic prose for Pervaneh and Rafi, were neither better nor worse in performance than the usual Oriental dithyrambs. Somehow, *Hassan*, instead of being the play of its age, became that spectacular "Eastern show" at His Majesty's. In an age of sliding panels Flecker's prose had one speech unexpectedly topical. "Did someone ask me," cried Rafi just before iron partitions fell with a crash, "why this house is called the House of the Moving Walls?"

Both the production of *Hassan* and its stage history were unexpected. Undoubtedly Marie Tempest's failure was an experience that this contained, poised technician of comediennes—poised usually over the tea-table—would find very rare indeed. For eight years she had been out of the London theatre, playing in America, touring in the East and the Antipodes, with her husband, W. Graham Browne. The return, in a "frivolous, inconsequent, frail" American comedy should have been a great West End occasion. Theatrical London was there to greet Marie Tempest on her first February night at the Duke of York's, some remembering her as she used to be in *Becky Sharp* and *Mrs. Dot* and *The Marriage of Kitty*; some going back to the years of musical comedy, *San Toy*, *The Geisha*, back even to *Dorothy*; and some—the youngest playgoers—come to consider a legend for the first time. It was a lost, limp farce; Marie Tempest, now employing every resource of her art—no one forgets the effect of those taut pauses, the half-turn of the head—could not begin to salvage it. Even so, it was startling to hear the gallery cry (against the play, not the actress) of "Rotten!" as she made her curtain speech. That was a disastrous beginning: *Good Gracious, Annabelle!*, alleged to be a romantic farce, ran for fifteen performances only, and though a revival of *The Marriage of Kitty*, which followed, did much better, it was plain that a dramatist must be found to match the artist: she could not live merely on the sympathetic affection of her public.

Another actress, another surprise. Tallulah Bankhead (her full name is Tallulah Brockman James Leicester Bankhead), Senator's daughter from Alabama, arrived at Wyndham's: a smouldering, pouting young woman with a voice like hot honey and milk, a face like an angry flower, eyes of violet-blue, and, at first, hair in a waving ash-blonde mane. (This was soon cut.) On chance she had come boldly to London from the Broadway theatre: her cheerful assurance, and the aid of Charles Cochran, got from a hypnotised Gerald du Maurier a part in the melodrama of *The Dancers*, which he and Viola Tree had written under the name of Hubert Parsons. The newcomer had some fierce little scenes that she acted with resolution and the magnetism that could all but draw her audiences upon the stage. The first-night house shouted for her (though it could not yet pronounce the name Tallulah), and it also enjoyed hearing Sir Gerald du Maurier observe to the nearest greaser, "Beat it, yellow streak!" The play could hardly have mattered less; but Tallulah Bankhead had acted herself into London, and for eight teeming years she was a West End cult, her followers ribboning out at the gallery doors thirty hours before any first performance.

Undeniably it was a year for actresses. Sybil Thorndike, with no fore-knowledge of *Saint Joan*, chose for some reason to play Imogen in *Cymbeline* after an early frivol in *Advertising April*, a farce by drama critics who were two of the wittiest writers of their time: Herbert Farjeon and Horace Horsnell. The full title of their anecdote about a film star (film stars were still surprising in 1923) was *Advertising April; or, The Girl Who Made the Sunshine Jealous*. Horsnell, in the autobiography he wrote in Augustan couplets—"this white elephant" as he inscribed it in the copy he gave to me—said of the collaboration with Farjeon:

> Their saucy satire has a movie theme:
> Good Business crowns creation's happy Dream:
> The Tragic Muse (who ne'er leaves things half done),
> Ingenious Sybil! finds their play good fun;

> And (Hecuba persuaded from her woes),
> She takes the stage in frills and furbelows.
> April's début (hidden from public sight)
> Her authors watch with unalloyed delight;
> Refrain, though pressed, to take a curtain call,
> And find that Fame comes lightly after all.

Audiences also found the play good fun. Imogen, whom many regard as Shakespeare's nonpareil, fared less well. (It was staged at the New Theatre; that autumn Sybil Thorndike and Tallulah Bankhead must often have met in the little courtyard between the stage doors of Wyndham's and the New.)

Cymbeline is a shining, shadowed play in which Snow White and Lear's Britain mix with the Renaissance. On the stage it either comes through magnificently, or not at all. In approaching Imogen, Sybil Thorndike—with all the flash and outbreak of her fiery mind—could not easily reduce pressure. Agate said: "She gives me the impression of having swallowed the character at one gulp, and of looking round the stage for something with which to be effective." Oddly, at the Birmingham Repertory early that year, Barry Jackson had presented *Cymbeline* (produced by H. K. Ayliff) in modern dress: an experiment of which much less was heard than the *Hamlet* in London two years later. But those were absorbing nights in Station Street. During the autumn a dazzling beam would rest on this theatre during the production of *Back to Methuselah*: I shall come to that in the London of 1924. The *Cymbeline* belonged wholly to Birmingham. The King, most thankless of title-rôles, wore an English Field-Marshal's uniform. Cloten was a lieutenant in the Brigade of Guards. Imogen, when disguised, wore schoolboy's knickerbockers and cap. Bache Matthews, the Repertory's earliest historian, recalled how the stage was darkened for the battle "which opened with the roar of artillery and the crackle of rifles, flashes from bursting shells revealing soldiers in khaki and steel helmets firing over an earthwork behind which they crouched until the bayonet charge of the Bersaglieri with their waving plumes".

Maybe if it had been done like this in London the New Theatre *Cymbeline* would have lasted longer than a month. That production was soon put aside so that Sybil Thorndike could act the woman who all but throttled a faithless sister in Henry Arthur Jones's drama, *The Lie*. The play, written several years earlier, was the last success of the seventy-two-year-old dramatist who once ruled the English drawing-room drama with Pinero, two kings upon one throne; and it is touching now to see how he dedicated the play to Sybil Thorndike, living again his final curtain-call: the moment when "under the shelter of your wing, myself moved by the inflaming sweep of your action, I stood beside you to acknowledge the prolonged acclamations".

There were many of these prolonged acclamations during 1923. They came for several different events. One was the English production of *R.U.R.*, or "Rossum's Universal Robots" ("Rossum" is Czech for reason). Here Karel Čapek, adding a word to the language, presented an uncompromising nightmare-drama of a world overwhelmed by its own creations. The scene —we note now with a certain quiver—is "An Island in the Year 1950". Not much resemblance there to, say, William Archer's *The Green Goddess*, a cunningly suave "thick-ear" play by the apparently austere theorist and translator of Ibsen, or Maugham's *Our Betters*, heartless comedy of a group of American expatriates (vicious circles, inconstant lovers), which had been acted in New York eight years earlier. Margaret Bannerman, the young Canadian actress who had been in the West End for some time with no special fortune, her *Decameron Nights* flutter aside, cut suddenly into the heart of Maugham's play with the diamond edge of her Pearl Grayston, a woman straight from the Restoration. She never did anything comparable.

First-night cheering echoes across from *Our Betters*. So it does also from Eugene O'Neill's *Anna Christie*, with Pauline Lord freely emotional as the lady of the barge, though Cochran lost on the venture, and in the fog scene the players' voices were blurred; from Coward's *The Young Idea* which did not run long, but brought its author in friendly touch with Cochran; and from *Aren't We All?* by the librettist of *The Maid of the Mountains* and *The Lady of the Rose*, Frederick Lonsdale. He had been for so many years a contented galley-slave of the libretto that everybody was surprised—in the spirit of the year— when he put up a comedy, in his later gilt-edged manner, about a serenely cynical peer resolved to reconcile his daughter-in-law and son: they are at war for the usual reasons, each being as guilty as the other. Hardly anyone realised during *Aren't We All?* that Lonsdale had, in fact, re-written his light comedy, *The Best People*, a short-runner of 1909. (Soon another dramatist would use that title, and Lonsdale's early play would be pushed farther towards oblivion.)

Whatever the provenance of *Aren't We All?*, Lonsdale was an important recruit to the legitimate theatre that badly needed new writers of staying power. (He kept his other hand in with the libretto of *Madame Pompadour* at Daly's.) C. K. Munro was a recruit: a Civil Servant and Ulsterman, writing under a pseudonym. Already he had offered one massive polemical discussion-play, *The Rumour*, fated—like various others in the years ahead—to be Sunday-night fodder for experimental production: work "for to admire and not to see". *At Mrs. Beam's*, put on for a run in 1923, was different. In it Munro chose to discuss that depressed area, the stage boarding-house. I said once that any dramatist troubled about construction can dump his cargo in a "Residents Only" lounge and have his easy fun and his easier drama. Munro had more originality; but the comedy proclaimed the fault that would blanket his career as a dramatist: the people talked too volubly, relentlessly. It is true that in *At Mrs. Beam's* the lavishly running-on dialogue is accurately keyed and phrased, and the imaginative Miss Shoe—whom Jean Cadell created with a peering, sustained zest—is never less than amusing. The play, with Dennis Eadie as a confidence trickster, ran almost as steadily as its dialogue. Yet, when it was performed by the Stage Society in 1921, a drama critic rated it so poorly that, a year later in a book of essays, he was talking of "a forgotten play", a play, we felt, in which Polonius had broken volubly loose and insisted on being the principal character in *Hamlet*. Where else? Drury Lane had a mediocre year with *Angelo*, a "romance of a great composer", tiresomely cinematic in method; a florid life of "Ned" Kean, who ought to be one of the Drury Lane ghosts; and *Good Luck*, an outmoded stick-at-nothing Druriodrama by Seymour Hicks and Ian Hay. Outmoded or not, it lasted for some time with a cast that included Convict 39 and Derek Vale, Earl of Trenton. Nobody talked about *What Money Can Buy* (Lyceum). Obviously, melodrama in the grand style was fraying, and the new thriller-school could not provide much. True, Sax Rohmer did his best. He wrote *The Eye of Siva*. We had to believe here—and why not?—that the Yellow Council of Seven proposed to destroy the white races by projecting through the eye of the god Siva a lightning-flash called the Smiling Death. It was daylight-clear that such a Council as this must be represented by a disguised Chinese mandarin. It was just as obvious that he would work from a Norfolk manor, and that there should be gathered in this house a Secret Service agent, an American Orientalist, an Indian butler, and a Manchurian leopardess.

Splendid: sheer naturalism. Ungratefully, playgoers let it fade after only eighty-seven performances, but some of the repertory theatres preserved it for a while, though the leopardess had to be taken on trust. London preferred *The Return of Sherlock Holmes*: Eille Norwood with violin and pipe (and tobacco in the toe of the Persian slipper), Watson in bone-headed amazement, and Lestrade woodenly intervening. It was practically Holmes's last case: he had kept some of his theatrical force.

We ought to look at half a dozen other productions—some of them surprising—from this year of medley before passing to what used to be called the lighter lyric stage. A word first about the Regent Theatre—long thrust to a cinema—which stood in Euston Road, close to three of the great rail termini: a useful position for any visitors from Scotland, the North, and the Midlands, who felt a consuming desire, as they travelled towards London, to pop over the road from the station and into *The Immortal Hour*. The Regent had been the Euston Palace of Varieties, re-named in compliment to Arnold Bennett— the Regent was the "Card's" theatre—and opened by Nigel Playfair in the summer of 1922 with Bennett's *Body and Soul*. This failed: it was then that Barry Jackson, of the Birmingham Repertory, entered as a London manager.

Already he had produced in Birmingham Rutland Boughton's opera of a shadowy world ("How beautiful they are, the lordly ones!") about the fairy princess who weds the High King of Ireland, and who is wooed back by Midir, the immortal, to her own realm. Then, in the autumn of 1922, Jackson brought the opera to the Regent, opening on a Friday the thirteenth. It was many months before *The Immortal Hour* was withdrawn; but it did less well than to-day—looking back into a rosy haze—we may imagine. In fact, Barry Jackson lost some thousands on the opera. When it became a cult playgoers went again and again, belatedly: it could not now be more than a *succès d'estime*. The trees in Paul Shelving's glimmering ancient forest haunt the mind; and the scarlet and blue and gold in the hall at Tara. Gwen Ffrangcon-Davies, the wandering Etain, made her name as a singer who was also an actress, rapt, visionary, ethereal, with nothing of the self-consciousness that had thickened the Celtic twilight. Any work that could have drawn Barry Jackson to London would have been welcomed. In 1958, when he is the most honoured elder statesman of the British stage, those November nights at the Regent are still high in recollection. "He is the Theatre," wrote a poet in 1953 at the fortieth birthday of the Birmingham Repertory.

He is the Theatre;
He has felt its power,
Through forty years, to kindle or to bless,
And he has deemed it, in all happiness,
Not forty years, but one Immortal Hour.

It was after Barry Jackson's season at the Regent that Nigel Playfair produced *The Insect Play*, a laboured bit of satirical symbolism by the Čapeks. It lingers in this record, curiously, because the part of the Poet Butterfly in the first scene was acted none too well by a young man in white flannels, pumps, a silk shirt, a green laurel-wreath, fair hair, and a gold battledore and shuttlecock. His name: John Gielgud. Printers took a dislike to the name and transformed it to Gillcud, Cielgud, and Grilgood. The actor was far happier in a small part (and also as Claude Rains's understudy) in *Robert E. Lee*, a grave and scrupulously restrained Drinkwater chronicle that kept the romantic quality of the general of the South. It surprises us to see that Gordon Harker, destined to be the hoarse, pint-of-bitter Cockney of so many West End plays, was Drinkwater's Jefferson Davis. Out in Waterloo Road the Royal Victoria Hall, *alias* the Old Vic, had the courage to try *Titus Andronicus* ("Murders, rapes, and massacres, acts of black night, abominable deeds") which would be immensely fashionable thirty years on: the theatre of the Gay Twenties knew nothing of *musique concrète*.

At the St. Martin's, in Charles McEvoy's *The Likes of 'Er*—a few years later Gordon Harker would assuredly have been in it—a child actress, Hermione Baddeley, flared across the stage in a scene for a passionate Cockney girl tamed into contrition after a clatter of crockery-smashing. Next door, at the Ambassadors, the much-loved Meggie Albanesi, whom John Masefield had said would be "the wonder of our stage", acted for the last time, in an amiable comedy, *The Lilies of the Field*. On December 9, at the age of 24, she died, leaving a memory of an artist who "died in the service of the theatre"— words inscribed on the plaque at the St. Martin's—and whose power to reach the heart has seldom been matched. John Galsworthy, after watching and listening to her as Sydney in *A Bill of Divorcement*, told her that she had established the girl "from the inside". At her death James Agate said: "You felt that she had not only thought out her parts, but fought them out within her own bosom. She was the first victim of that pity and terror which it is the

59. "What, frighted with false fire!": the Play scene from the modern-dress production of *Hamlet* at the Kingsway Theatre, 1925.

60. A slave-market hallucination: the fugitive "Emperor's" terror in the forest: Paul Robeson in *The Emperor Jones* at the Ambassadors Theatre, 1925.

61. The voluble widow, Mrs. Madigan: Maire O'Neill as the neighbour in *Juno and the Paycock* at the Royalty Theatre, 1925.

62. Lady Frinton: "Come, come, young woman! What is your usual charge for the return of letters?" Mrs. Cheyney: "Speaking as 'one fallen woman' to another, there have never been any letters": round the table in the third act of *The Last of Mrs. Cheyney* at the St. James's Theatre, 1925, are Mabel Sealby, May Whitty, Gladys Gray, Ellis Jeffreys, Ronald Squire, Gladys Cooper, Dawson Milward, Gerald du Maurier, and Basil Loder.

63. "Emmet Carr in the Flat of the Siren": Francis Lister and Olga Lindo in the American play, *Tarnish*, Vaudeville, 1925.

64. Tallulah Bankhead as Iris Fenwick, the heroine of Michael Arlen's play, *The Green Hat*, at the Adelphi Theatre, 1925.

65. Prince: "Oh, Katja, you're wonderful." "Miss Davies's cloak and dresses designed and made by Idare et Cie, 78 Wigmore St., W." Lilian Davies as Katja Karina and Gregory Stroud as Prince Carl of Koruja in *Katja the Dancer* at the Gaiety Theatre, 1925.

66. "Your usual, miss?"—"One must kick sometimes, mustn't one?"—"There's a kick in that, miss; I mixed it myself." Evelyn Laye and Cecil Fowler in *Betty in Mayfair* at the Adelphi Theatre, 1925.

67. Joe Coyne, Binnie Hale, and George Grossmith made their audiences happy for 665 performances in *No, No, Nanette* at the Palace Theatre, 1925.

68. *Rose Marie* at Drury Lane, 1925: Totem Pole Lodge, near Kootenay Pass in the Canadian Rockies. Song and dance: "Totem Tom Tom." Wanda (Mira Nirska) and Chorus of Totem Poles.

69. Leonard Hornsey conducts the London Hippodrome orchestra and the chorus of *Mercenary Mary*, 1925, in "Dipping in the Moonlight."

privilege of the artist to evoke." In Shakespearian phrase—Meggie Albanesi had no chance to play in Shakespeare—death lay on her like an untimely frost, upon the sweetest flower of all the field.

A few days before her death she had been to the fantasy for which the year 1923 may be honoured: Vane Sutton Vane's *Outward Bound*. It distressed Meggie Albanesi: "A strange influence," she told her mother, "that has upset me so much." Many who prize *Outward Bound* must wish to keep it as they knew it first. It was by an actor-dramatist who had written little of value before, and who would do nothing comparable. Here he imagined a morality of a Ship of the Dead. Its first act is upon the rim of the unknown. A variety of people find themselves in "a room which suggests rather than represents the large smoke-room of a small ocean liner". They cannot tell why they are on board. One by one, as the ominously quiet ship sails on, they reveal their characters in closely-judged dialogue, superficially matter-of-fact but with a haunting overtone. Ultimate revelation must come. It does at the end of the act when a young drunkard gathers the truth in a few words with the steward Scrubby, who stands, in Sutton Vane's pattern, for Charon, ferryman of the Styx. The moment is a freak of the mind:

"We are—now answer me truthfully—we are all *dead*, aren't we?"
A pause. Scrubby answers very quietly:
"Yes, sir; we are all dead. They don't find out so soon as you have as a rule."

Outward Bound is consistent and unforced to the end. Its last Judgment scene is neither pompous nor petty: it could so easily have been both.

Just four weeks after this, an audience in the Birmingham Repertory Theatre—Shaw himself was there—heard Lilith speaking the epilogue to the metabiological pentateuch of *Back to Methuselah*: "Of life only is there no end . . .' Within a few months *Methuselah* would come to London. The gallant surprise at Birmingham spoke nobly for Barry Jackson's faith. Cedric Hardwicke, the He-Ancient in *As Far As Thought Can Reach*, described the cycle as [a great spiritual adventure. He remembered, too, an old lady, a regular Repertory subscriber, who complained to the box-office that she hated acrobatics of any kind, and trick cyclists in particular.

The provinces would depend more and more upon its expanding complex of Repertory Theatres: places, said St. John Ervine, where all intelligent persons may find intelligent recreation, rather than places where melancholy

men and misunderstood women may twiddle their souls. The touring list
remained very long; but already (with the cinema's prosperity rising) it had
begun, though slowly, to decrease. As yet the dingy small revue had not
noticeably suffered: an odd breed of stock-pot production of which, at that
hour, some 200 were on the road: "hurrying, scurrying comedy revues",
"non-stop laugh shows", "colossal riots", "super-screams". The titles were
merely interchangeable tags (*Gin Fizz, Flutters and Spangles*). Patriotic melodramas had disappeared. Instead, songs of Araby were sung in a Highland
setting; Venice and Venezuela outstretched frightened hands; one Colossal
Riot in Fifteen Sumptuous Scenes followed the next, each with a set-piece of
Cuba or sunny Seville, and with its broad comedian compact of slapstick and
innuendo. There were touring frolics of the better sort—the young Gracie Fields
had her training in the veteran *Mr. Tower of London*—but the skimble-skamble
stuff, the lesser lunacies, the anonymous nondescripts have sunk without trace.

In London the light musical stage was approaching a new day. The old,
high-romantic Never-Never land of Daly's and the Gaiety, its Ruritanian-
Cadonian pomp, its baronial banter, its balladry and banditry, was dimming.
The fashion was for "dancing shoes with nimble soles". Everywhere the
theatre sought fresh manners and methods, and within its restless orbit
musical comedy was perhaps the most restless medium of all. The older
school would exist for a while. James White, the magnate who had been a
bricklayer in Rochdale, backed the Viennese *Madame Pompadour* at Daly's,
with Evelyn Laye and music by Leo Fall. And *Catherine*, at the Gaiety, with
José Collins married to Peter the Great in the last act and three supporters
needed to carry her wedding dress, was an attempt to do with Tschaikowsky
what *Lilac Time* had done with Schubert. It was a debatable business, even if
one critic, applauding it, said: "In the temper of the public there was not a
single dissonant. From the introduction to the finale—a fragment of '1812'
with the National Hymn of Russia interwoven—the house gave free rein to
its enthusiasm, that grew to ecstasy, almost to paroxysm." Maybe; but
Catherine lasted for a mere 217 performances. The new musical play was
coming, and for the old it could be only a procession of protracted death.

There were hints this year of the new order: in the American *Little Nelly
Kelly*, brought across by Cochran, and with no song-hit now that lingers; and,
more urgently, in *Stop Flirting*. There, in an otherwise unremarkable romp,
the American brother and sister, Fred and Adèle Astaire, danced themselves

into London with that jog-trot, "The Whichness of the Whatness". Fred Astaire was also to coach Noël Coward in dancing. This determined young man, after declaring that to appear in a revue might injure his prestige as a straight actor, contrived briskly to get himself cast as leading juvenile of *London Calling!*, the revue of which he was part-author. ("It was a tremendous success . . . the Press was almost unanimous over one thing, and that was that I should never have been allowed to appear in it.") The Sitwell family, a little troubled by Coward's treatment of a family of poets, the Whittlebots (Maisie Gay as Hernia Whittlebot) appeared to be unanimous that Coward should never have been allowed to write it. However, *London Calling!* was indeed a "tremendous success", with Gertrude Lawrence and Noël Coward singing a duet, "You Were Meant for Me,"[1] and Gertrude Lawrence alone acting "Early Mourning" with "verisimilitude worthy of Maupassant".

One more flash from 1923. Cochran, at this stage as idealistic as unfortunate, presented Eleonora Duse for a few London matinées. Also he brought to the Pavilion an Anglo-American revue, *Dover Street to Dixie*. The first half was white; the second coloured, a "plantation revue", with Will Vodery's coloured orchestra. The evening had pattered on so dully that everything rested upon the Dixie half. Presently Florence Mills came on, without parade, to sing a plaintive song of Tennessee. She had scarcely begun before her listeners strained forward, hushed. "She owns the house," Cochran whispered to his companion. "No audience in the world can resist that." The audience did not resist. Thereafter, at the Pavilion, the house would applaud Florence Mills *before* every song she sang. Somebody compared her to a plaintive stick of dynamite: "One moment we are weeping; then we are all in mid-air together." London would certainly meet her again.

Postscript: London would not meet again *If Winter Comes*, a dramatisation of A. S. M. Hutchinson's best-selling novel of the period. It ran for fifty-three performances at the St. James's. We remember Owen Nares, but who in the world now was Mark Sabre? The novel of which he was the hero had inspired two songs during the previous year. Melville Gideon sang one in *The Co-Optimists*. The other, "If Winter Comes, Summer Will Come Again," had a lyric by Reginald Arkell. From the theatre of the Fifties we stare incredulously at the composer's name. It was H. M. Tennent.

---

[1] By Sissle and Blake. Called "I Was Meant for You" in the first-night programme, a title used again in the film *Broadway Melody*, 1929.

VI

1924

"We are a great people for labels, and we furnish them with wellnigh imperishable gum," wrote Hilton Brown. If I must go on labelling the Gay Twenties—though my gum has to be spread tentatively—I would call 1924 the Historical Year. It brought, in Bernard Shaw's *Saint Joan*, the most enduring work of the decade; in *The Vortex*, the most immediately contentious, a *Look Back in Anger* of its time; in *The Farmer's Wife*, one of London's longest runs; in *Havoc*, the first serious war scenes to hold a West End theatre; and in *A Midsummer Night's Dream*, the return of Shakespeare to Drury Lane.

Saint Joan was London's second Shaw play of the year, or—on a recount —his sixth, for Barry Jackson had put on at the Court, during the spring, the five sections of *Back to Methuselah*. (Edith Evans, occupied with Congreve's Millamant, could not wear the Serpent's hood and glistening green and purple scales in the first of them, Eden's bower in flower.) The plays were received with a complicated blend of adoration, nervous respect, and loud mocking bravado. They are a tireless union of intellect and imagination, but it may be that their future home is the study. When Jackson first resolved to do them in Birmingham, Shaw fired off a postcard, "Mr. Jackson, are your wife and children provided for?" To-day only the first and fifth have any special preservative quality in the theatre. *In the Beginning*, Shaw's vast parable of Creative Evolution, shines into radiance beneath the first dayspring: the pure, bright colours of Paul Shelving's set are untarnished in memory. At the last (A.D. 31,920), *As Far As Thought Can Reach*, Shavian prose achieves its gravest harmonies, and Lilith—voiced with a timeless dignity by Margaret Chatwin —rises from the dark to look to a day when Man's will has conquered, when the final stream between flesh and spirit has been forded, and life (world without end) is a glory of pure intellect, the "vortex freed from matter".

Before *Saint Joan* appeared at the New, *Back to Methuselah* had yielded at the Court to a play that was probably as big (indeed as rash) a contrast as anyone could have devised: *The Farmer's Wife* by the Dartmoor novelist, Eden Phillpotts. (He was also a dramatist but his plays had lacked staying-power; he had forgotten many of their titles.) *The Farmer's Wife*, written twelve years earlier, had been performed at Birmingham—where it was a popular show-piece—in 1916: on that occasion A. E. Drinkwater, father of John Drinkwater the poet, directed it.

Now it was to stay in London for 1,329 performances: a record then exceeded only twice in a world that had never heard of *The Mousetrap*, *Worm's Eye View*, and *Blithe Spirit*. At the time I write, its endeared author, who was ninety-five in November 1957, has managed to avoid seeing his comedy in performance. I think he has missed something. In our day *The Farmer's Wife* is praised as a rule—glum juniors find it too happy, too idyllic—for its portrait of Churdles Ash, the old hind who is as thorough-paced a misogynist as Strindberg, with a rather different way of expressing himself. His first words are: "There's marriage in the air, Araminta, and us that have escaped the state be often quickest to see the fatal signs." A gnarled, nubbly crab-apple, Churdles, in retrospect, controls the stage, though his part is far smaller than we imagine. The farcical comedy is about a widowed and eligible farmer's search for a wife, his dealings with three possible candidates —"You are the first man, dear Samuel Sweetland, who has accepted my sex challenge," says Thirza Tapper—and the inevitable discovery that Araminta Dench, his own housekeeper, waits for him. It is most sturdily and amusingly wrought. Phillpotts is never up from Mummerset; his speech can flow like the "travelling musics" (as Sir John Squire has called them) of the moorland streams. No dramatist of the period has babbled better of green fields. They said on the London hoardings, "The Farmer's Wife is the Laugh of Your Life." Playgoers speak yet of Cedric Hardwicke's Churdles—Hardwicke was one of a quite unknown cast—as he announced "My lot!" with that thumb-twitch over his shoulder. The performance has been magnified in memory until it fills the Little Silver sky. Hardwicke's laundress, on being offered passes, told him afterwards that she was most ashamed; although she enjoyed the play very much, it was all she could do to keep from laughing.

We are puzzled now to reflect that when, a fortnight after *The Farmer's Wife* première, *Saint Joan* reached the West End, some people could not refrain from mocking laughter. Not at the performance itself—that was a triumph—but afterwards. Shaw throughout life had alienated many by his candid use of what he called "the cart and the trumpet". Hence there was a certain amount of malicious, sour-grapes comment on *Saint Joan*. Its heroine was a pillar of faith and fire, *alias* what Shaw, in his usual capricious Preface, called "the queerest fish among the eccentric worthies of the Middle Ages". Generally, Joan of Arc in the theatre had meant some flamboyant chronicle skirmish with a terrific melodramatic to-do—*Wandering Jew* fashion—round the stake at Rouen. But Shaw's *Joan* never loitered for a minute in Wardour Street. Here was a country girl from the Vosges, using a country accent and stripped of the conventional blazonry. The last words of the Epilogue, when Sybil Thorndike paused, for a moment only, in that silver gleam in which Joan is enshrined in the hearts of France, went at once into stage history: "O God that madest this beautiful earth, when will it be ready to receive Thy saints? How long, O Lord, how long?"

Sybil Thorndike, who played Joan with an ecstasy no one has yet approached—though the passing years have brought to us Celia Johnson and Siobhan McKenna—has said of the hotly-argued Epilogue: "It was sadly misunderstood at the first production, but it shows how a prophet can make ideas grow, for nowadays that Epilogue is accepted almost universally as a necessary part of the shape. Those who feel that G. B. S. is just coldly reasonable should read again the great litany of the poor human sinners who had been actors in the drama." The Thorndike Joan was at once the armoured Maid, the girl-warrior whose voice is "bright, strong, and rough", and the "poor innocent child of God" who is Saint Joan. (History will have less to record of two Joan of Arc plays that were rushed on immediately in the deeper provinces, one including among its characters the Chevalier Gaston Falconbridge and a Vision of St. Michael.)

Shaw's year, some named it. Truly it was a belated high summer for the dramatist who, though he was sixty-seven, had several years to go before he was a figure accepted as Venerable and Blessed. It was also, in another degree, Noël Coward's year. In November he went to the draughty and austere little Everyman, on the heights of Hampstead, in the drama of *The Vortex*, greeted just as John Osborne's invective would be greeted during 1956. Most decades throw up their angry, articulate, and theatrically-minded young men, and Coward had a thoroughly good time when he exposed the follies of Mayfair, the sins of society, in a plot for which the day's modish adjective was "hectic". In the last act of his play, by no means a "vortex freed from matter", Coward and Lilian Braithwaite, as son and mother, had a modern variation on the Closet Scene of *Hamlet*. Florence, saying "You're neurotic and ridiculous . . . you come and say wicked, cruel things to me", was just as much the Gertrude of a 1924 Mayfair, as Nicky ("I've seen you make a vulgar, disgusting scene in your own house") was a very modern young Hamlet. Coward believed intensely in his own part, all dope and crashing piano-chords. On the first night at the Everyman his acting was strung tighter than any violin-string. The première had come shakily into being out of the usual glorious theatrical muddle. Towards the end, Coward cut a vein in his wrist when he swept the cosmetics and bottles off the dressing-table with a grand gesture. "I bound it up with my handkerchief during the curtain-calls, but it bled effectively throughout my author's speech."

A month later, and the play was on in the West End: Coward had begun in earnest the career that would make of him not only the chosen dramatist of the Twenties, but also one of the most prolific writers in the modern theatre. Somerset Maugham said of him: "He knocked at the door with impatient knuckles, and then he rattled the handle, and then he burst in. After a moment's stupor the older playwrights welcomed him affably enough and retired with what dignity they could muster to the shelf which, with a sprightly gesture, he indicated to them as their proper place."

Another prolific dramatist who yet had only one West End production was a Yorkshire solicitor, Harry Wall. I doubt whether his name will ring any bells to-day; but he ought to be honoured as the man who first brought to the West End theatre a harshly real picture of trench warfare. Until that time audiences knew nothing of the muddy trench, the "rainy marching in the painful field", the humours of the dug-out, the prose gallantries of the front line. Harry Wall's *Havoc*, which had been refused by ten managers, might have been melodramatic in scheme, but it was clear that its central acts, in a Flanders dug-out, had stirred him as they stirred the audience on an early spring night at the Haymarket Theatre. Sir George Arthur, who was at the première, relates how, after the scene in which a young subaltern called "the Babe" was brought into the dug-out, half-demented by his first experience of the horror of desperate hand-to-hand fighting, the curtain rose thirty-five times to the cheering of an audience overwhelmed. The actor was Richard Bird, later to be a distinguished West End producer. "Some day, perhaps," wrote James Agate, "Mr. Bird will read how the pit rose at this or that actor of the past. I imagine he will look back with pride to the fact that, once at least in his own life, he had that recognition which is the actor's supreme reward." Henry Kendall, afterwards both a producer and a resourceful light comedian, played in *Havoc* a blinded major betrayed by a singularly heartless vamp. For a few months this piece fixed public attention. Unhappily, there was less applause for a better play, *The Conquering Hero*, by Allan Monkhouse, who had been one of the drama critics of the *Manchester Guardian* in Manchester. It is the tragedy of a soldier who goes unwillingly to war, who finds humiliation in France, and who returns to the bitter ironies of a triumphant welcome home. This is not a semi-documentary play; it is a flight of the spirit.

We could not have used that term about many other plays of the year: Galsworthy's *Old English*, for example, which lived on its portrait of a stoical freebooter (inevitably a Norman McKinnel part) and had some uncommonly feeble humour: "I bet he's got the dead rat down his back by now. And isn't it niffy!" There was little for the spirit in the appalling American "glad girl" comedy, *Pollyanna*, one of the treacliest inventions that had smeared itself across London (Pollyanna kissed the old-clothes barrel after observing "I love every stitch you've ever given me"); or in Lonsdale's unlooked-for melo-drama, *The Fake*, one of his rare ventures outside the neo-Restoration play; or in *Conchita*, a muddle in which Tallulah Bankhead, when a monkey with stage-fright snatched her wig at the première, threw a despairing cartwheel; or in *The Royal Visitor*, an over-dressed, under-written, over-cast comedy from the French, that had nine performances at His Majesty's; or in a sultry seduction play, *Fata Morgana*, from the Hungarian; or even in the enchant-ingly mad American farce, *It Pays to Advertise* ("Thirteen Soap—Unlucky for Dirt") which ranks as the second in the Aldwych series. Ben Travers was soon to knock at the door, though without Coward's impatient knuckles.

I must include four melodramas of the year. One, a wholly egregious pin-the-villain play, *The Lure*, I cherish from a provincial production a few months later, when the villain tapped his waistcoat and snarled at the heroine: "Don't struggle! I've locked the key, and the door is in my pocket." Another, and an oddity then as now, was *The Rat* by David L'Estrange, a pseudonym that hid, not too efficiently, Constance Collier and Ivor Novello. It was madly theatri-cal smash-and-grab about a grease-painted, Apache-haunted Paris, that was livelier at least than Galsworthy's rat, and would pant on through the years in touring productions that would have much surprised Mr. L'Estrange.

70. The ubiquitous Dodge Twins (Betty and Beth) in *Turned Up* at the New Oxford Theatre, 1926.

71. Anton Dolin as Little Boy Blue in his ballet to Elgar's music, London Coliseum, 1926. His partner is Ninette de Valois.

72. "A Tragedy of Fashion, or The Scarlet Scissors": danced in Nigel Playfair's revue, *Riverside Nights*, at the Lyric, Hammersmith, 1926. "Story by Ashley Dukes, music by Eugene Goossens, choreography by Frederick Ashton, decorated by F.E.D." It was danced by Elizabeth Vincent, Frederick Ashton, Marie Rambert, Esmé Biddle, Earle Grey, and Frances James.

73. Violet Dunn (heroine), caught by villain (Bernard Nedell), and rescued by hero (Roy Lloyd), in *Broadway*, the American cabaret-comedy-drama, Adelphi, 1926.

74. "Meester Bob—it all right if Aloma stay here to-night. Aloma promise she not tell Missionary in the morning." Vivienne Osborne and Francis Lister in *Aloma*, Adelphi, 1926.

75. Tallulah Bankhead (Jerry) rejects the millionaire, Barney Barnett (Charles Carson), in *The Gold Diggers* at the Lyric Theatre, 1926.

76. The Prologue to Galsworthy's *Escape*, Ambassadors Theatre, 1926: Matt Denant (Nicholas Hannen) chats with the Girl of the Town (Ursula Jeans) in Hyde Park.

77. "Flags for the Lifeboat?": from the stairs and across, Ena Mason (as the flag-seller), Mary Brough, Sydney Lynn, Vera Gerald, Ethel Coleridge, Robertson Hare, Stella Bonheur, Ralph Lynn, Tom Walls, Griffith Humphreys and Winifred Shotter in *Rookery Nook* at the Aldwych Theatre, 1926.

78. *The Constant Nymph*, New Theatre, 1926: The musical party in the drawing room at Strand-on-the-Green: Lewis Dodd (Noel Coward), at the piano, startles Tessa (Edna Best) and the assembled company.   Keneth Kent and Cathleen Nesbitt are standing beside the central divan.

79. In *Princess Charming* (Palace Theatre, 1926), Princess Elaine of Novia (Winnie Melville) is forced by a local revolution to marry Captain Torelli, of the Sylvanian Navy (John Clarke), as the only means of escaping death. She does so in the presence of King Christian of Sylvania (George Grossmith) and the Attorney-General (Ernest Graham).

80. Ivy Tresmand, in the title-rôle of *Yvonne*, at Daly's Theatre, 1926, is surrounded by her admirers.

81. Marjorie Robertson (who was to become known as Anna Neagle), Harry Webster, Jean Perrie, and Noranna Rose dance *A Tragedy in the Chicken Run*, "a feature in the new Supper Show, *Merry-Go-Round*, at the Trocadero," 1926.

82. Nigel Playfair's ill-fated "review", *The Midnight Follies* at the Hotel Metropole, 1926. "It was quite evident," he said, "that the young ladies of the chorus thought very little of my entertainment."

83. Mrs. Pepys (Yvonne Arnaud) makes her husband (Edmund Gwenn) swear that he will never look at a pretty woman again: a scene from *And So To Bed* at the Queen's Theatre, 1926.

84. Peter Standish (Lawrence Anderson) meets his ancestors, Helen (Jean Forbes-Robertson), Lady Anne (Beatrice Wilson), Tom (Brian Gilmour), Kate (Valerie Taylor), and Throstle (Ivor Barnard), in *Berkeley Square* at the St. Martin's, 1926.

85. Paul Shelving's Devon village: Ralph Richardson, Viola Lyel, Cedric Hardwicke, Edward Petley, Susan Richmond, Muriel Hewitt, and Frank Vosper in *Yellow Sands* at the Haymarket Theatre, 1926.

("I'm afraid we have a success," reported Ivor Novello's chauffeur to Constance Collier after the first night of the try-out; and it went on being a success, tuppence-coloured to the end.) A third play, *White Cargo*, was Leon Gordon's sultry idea of home life on the West Coast of Africa. It introduced the phrase "mammy-palaver" to London, and whenever I hear the title now, there flashes before me the portico of a great provincial theatre covered with posters that announce "A Vivid Play of the Primitive, Unvarnished Life of the Tropics". The most primitive and unvarnished part of it was the black temptress, Tondeleyo, reeling and writhing and fainting in coils. No one who saw it in London will have forgotten Mary Clare's scream of fear, or Franklin Dyall as the quinine-bitter Weston. When *White Cargo* reached its 500th birthday, Dyall had not missed a single performance.

I choose the last melodrama, a sulky, spitting, clawing affair, a very Tondeleyo of a play, *Tiger Cats*, because the predatory vampire (a "Serpent woman who revels in her power over man") was one of the parts Edith Evans acted during 1924. The year put her beside Sybil Thorndike at the head of their profession. Consider it. During the spring, in Congreve's *The Way of the World*, London heard, at the Lyric, Hammersmith, the tones of the only true Millamant of her period: the voice with its fan spread and streamers out, a darting, flashing, swallow-flight of a voice. Edith Evans was the Restoration reborn. Playfair's revival, as I have said, must have annoyed readers impatient with any form of drama criticism that was not a banquet of sloes and powdered glass: the entire Press rose at Edith Evans. During the summer she had her thrust at the tigress Suzanne. In September, at *Back to Methuselah* matinées, she used the "strange, seductively musical whisper" of the Serpent from beneath its amethystine hood. And in December, and at Drury Lane, she had one of her less fortunate parts, a small-scale Helena in Basil Dean's revival of *A Midsummer Night's Dream*, one of the last productions of Shakespeare in the old, excessively elaborate method. Its company, then with some experiments, now sounds to us all-star. Basil Dean, an unmatched realistic producer, who had been Tree's stage-manager at His Majesty's, had organised precisely this sequence of detailed pictures. Fokine had prepared the ballets; there was full bounty of Mendelssohn, and the evening lasted four hours. It seemed to follow naturally that the verse suffered from a "restless and ambitious spectacle".

There had been simpler Shakespearian productions that year. At the

E

Old Vic Ion Swinley, the classical actor who possessed everything except a stable memory, was a Hamlet with rare nobility of mind, voice, and presence. Among the artists of his generation he was the potential leader who never led, the great might-have-been of the British stage. And out at the Regent Theatre a Romeo that one critic diagnosed as "unduly consumptive", partnered the child-Juliet of Gwen Ffrangcon-Davies. The actor was John Gielgud, better cast than as the Poet Butterfly. By now the printers had a firm hold of his name. Earlier he had had a letter of some charm from his agent: "If you would like to play the finest lead among the plays by the late William Shakespeare, will you please call upon Mr. Peacock and Mr. Ayliff at the Regent Theatre on Friday at 2.30 p.m. Here is an opportunity to become a London Star in a night. Please confirm." Mr. Gielgud confirmed; but though he spoke Romeo's verse with a passion that set him, vocally, in the proper period, it would not be his historical year. He and Mr. Akerman May would have been surprised to know that, nearly a quarter of a century later, a bold, trampling fellow—oh, a very devil—after hearing *Romeo and Juliet* at Stratford-upon-Avon, would dismiss the tragedy as "mawkish, confused, improbable, and sluggish".

It was a better year for devotees of the Russian Ballet. Diaghilev in November came back to the Coliseum, his quarrel with Sir Oswald Stoll resolved. One gathered that Harry Tate's presence was needed whenever a music-hall turned to the classics. He had been in the evening bill at the Holborn Empire when Sybil Thorndike acted Greek tragedy there at matinées; now at the Coliseum he was giving the same act, "Fishing", when Diaghilev returned, and London met for the first time Cocteau's ballet *Le Train Bleu*, planned to show off the fantastically agile acrobatic dancing of Anton Dolin (Patrick Healey-Kay) as Le Beau Gosse. It was not presented again after Dolin left the company. Such famous dancers as Nijinska, Tchernicheva, Sokolova (*née* Hilda Munnings), Woizikowsky, Balanchine, Lifar, and Ninette de Valois were among Diaghilev's names. During this season, and in 1925, the Ballet danced at the Coliseum for the last time. The famous *Sleeping Princess* (*La Belle au Bois Dormant*) was only a memory—with its gold fire of autumn in the Bakst hunting scene—but a suggestion of past glory remained in *Aurora's Wedding*, a set of dances from the last act of *The Sleeping Princess*, with some additions. The stored Bakst scenery, which Stoll had released, had been ruined by damp; still one backcloth remained intact and it was

used in the divertissement as a token of greatness past. Another famous figure
of ballet had been seen for a month in the autumn of 1924 on the stage of
Covent Garden. This was Anna Pavlova, of whose Giselle, so imaginatively
heightened, *The Times* said: "Curtain-fall leaves us wondering how all that
elaboration of rhythmic movement could adapt itself so perfectly to such
diverse romantic ends." (It was during this season that the R.S.P.C.A. sent
an inspector to examine complaints about the emaciated horse, Rosinante, of
Don Quixote, a tribute to its careful make-up.)

The "lighter people", in Malvolio's disparaging phrase, had an indifferent year. José Collins, red-wigged at the Gaiety, turned herself loyally
into Nell Gwynne in a British musical play, cosily entitled *Our Nell*, another
effort to teach the historians what they had forgotten. It had been adapted
from an earlier piece that celebrated Peg Woffington. *Our Peg, Our Nell*, it
did not really matter. A critic discerned only one line of wit. "We are not
unmindful," said Charles, "that a king is the father of his people." "Of many
of them, sire," said Rochester. W. H. Berry, in *Poppy* at the same theatre,
battered at a glum libretto. A so-called "fantastic ballad-opera", *Kate ;
or, Love Will Find Out the Way*, remained fantastic for a brief run undisturbed
by the public. *Patricia* (specimen joke: "I believe in theories, I'm a theo-
dolite") and *Primrose* ran usefully, but their charms have withered. In *The
Street Singer* Frederick Lonsdale took another holiday from the straight drama
to write a libretto, with music by Harold Fraser-Simson. It was more substantial than some. "Phyllis Dare," reported James Agate, "received an
ovation never accorded to Bernhardt, Duse, or Ellen Terry, and which Miss
José Collins herself might have deemed adequate." *Toni*, at the Shaftesbury
Theatre, was a dancers' musical play, and Jack Buchanan and June—the
Princess's tiara so low on her forehead that it almost bumped her nose—swept
through it at speed.

Oceans and continents lay between this method of production and
Midsummer Madness at Playfair's Hammersmith. Clifford Bax, who wrote the
"comedy for music" (the music was by Armstrong Gibbs), hoped that it
might "please my fellows like a print from Watteau". It had a cast of four,
two of whom were Marie Tempest and Frederick Ranalow. Marie Tempest
was in her sixties; she had not sung in a theatre for eight years; it was nearly
two decades since she had acted in a musical play, and she would not do so
again. But at Hammersmith, and goldenly, she resumed her past. A special

song had been written for her, "Neglected Moon", and she was so startled by the affectionate length of the ovation that she "mislaid her voice" during the last speeches of the play, and Frederick Ranalow had to improvise.

That production was exceptional. We have finally to return from it to the revues of the year: names only, though ghoulish collectors of the stage failure will think of the booing of Lee White and Clay Smith in *Come In* ("I've been stung," said someone; "So have we!" retorted the gallery). More cheerfully, there was the massive, cut-and-come-again fooling of Maisie Gay in *Charlot's Revue*, especially when, as "Miss Fancy Robinson", to the accompaniment of a grand piano on the stage, and with a bunch of property flowers and a never-used gold chair, she sang such ballads (by Noël Coward) as "A Little Slut of Six" and "The Girls I am Leaving in England To-day". From this year we can take also the musical act of Norah Blaney and the nonchalant Gwen Farrar in *The Punch Bowl*; the singing Australian sisters, Lorna and Toots Pounds, all plumes and ostrich feathers in the Palladium's *Whirl of the World*; a complicated line from a Kingsway revue, *Yoicks!*, "If port exists at all, then, logically, it must once have been what it was"; the young Hermione Baddeley and Gilbert Childs in the wry comedy of their "Missing the Bus" sketch in *The Co-Optimists*; and Miss Baddeley's later appearance in *The Punch Bowl* that worried those who had seen in her the makings of a major "legitimate" artist: "More latent capacity," mourned Agate, "than any young actress living."

Agate, who insisted more sternly than anyone upon precision, should have been pleased this year by the tale of *Alf's Button*, which came to the Princes at Christmas, with Tubby Edlin as the pleasant, rueful-meek soldier with a talisman for summoning the djinn. W. A. Darlington, then (as he is, happily, to-day) drama critic of *The Daily Telegraph*, had adapted the play from his own extremely funny fantastic novel. When he wrote that, he had been taking, with acute perseverance, a course in Arabic, and the Arabic names and local colour of *Alf*, book and play, were accuracy itself. It seems that, at one point, Darlington might have become Professor of Persian (of which he did not know a word) at the University of Lahore. Fortunately for the English theatre, he stayed at home.

VII

1925

It is halfway through the Gay Twenties, and we have reached what is labelled somewhere as "a year of prodigious activity". Prodigious may be the word; as we gaze back at it, it seems to have been a year of strain. Each new week was resolved to go one better. Excitements flared and fell like spent matches; as soon as they were out, others appeared. There was no plan, not even a pencil-sketch of a pattern. The tempo of production had increased. *No, No, Nanette* was the swiftest musical play yet. Elsewhere, there was more and more reliance upon dancing. The musical-comedy theatre was a world of youth: it needed stamina now to sustain the pace.

Cochran, after a year's absence, was back at the Pavilion with revues named, topically, *On With the Dance* and *Still Dancing*. The legitimate theatre imported a great many American plays and rejected most of them at sight: it did not follow that what went on Broadway must be the toast of Shaftesbury Avenue. Ireland sent over a masterpiece of the day and age, *Juno and the Paycock*, by a former Dublin labourer, Sean O'Casey. The only English dramatists to write anything more than transient were Ashley Dukes, with his romantic Regency comedy, *The Man With a Load of Mischief*; Lonsdale, with *The Last of Mrs. Cheyney*, which has since survived a back-dated "Edwardian" revival; Coward, with the quick kingfisher-gleam of *Hay Fever*; and Ben Travers with the mad flurry of *A Cuckoo in the Nest* which proved that the moon was made of green cheese.

Timidly, at first, then excitedly, London discovered Chekhov. The experimental theatres and producing societies poured out their plays, and the Gate Theatre Studio (Peter Godfrey and Molly Veness) was born, behind a sacking curtain, on the upper floor of a warehouse near Covent Garden. John Barrymore acted Hamlet at the Haymarket (and might, he said, "have quit the theatre that same night, had it not been for the sake of Winston

Churchill"). There was a sudden roar of debate, with startled cheers and scandalised groans, when Sir Barry Jackson, knighted that spring, staged *Hamlet* in modern dress at the Kingsway. And to-day's reader, combing the massed programmes, will notice in the small print of the Casson-Thorndike *Henry the Eighth* at the Empire, Leicester Square, two days before Christmas, the entry: "Second Serving Man—Laurence Olivier". The same actor also appeared among a mixed bag of "Bishops, Lords, Officers, Guards, Scribes, etc."

Where to begin, then, in this fevered year when Shakespeare, New York, Maiden Blotton, Chekhov's Russia and Coward's Cookham, seem to move to the lilt of "I want to be happy"? Surely, at *No, No, Nanette* itself. It was the most famous musical play of its time and its world: what *Oklahoma!* would be to the Forties and *My Fair Lady* to the Fifties. One could hardly move without hearing somewhere one of the numbers by Vincent Youmans, the flickering see-saw of "Tea for Two", or the insistent note of "I want to be happy, But I won't be happy Till I've made you happy, too." Herbert Clayton and Jack Waller used their profits from the Aldwych farce, *It Pays to Advertise*, to present *Nanette* at the Palace. It was based, as we have seen, upon an obscure farce derived from a story, *Oh, James!* by May Edginton. Hawtrey had played the part that Joseph Coyne, long ago the Danilo of *The Merry Widow* and the Tony Chute of *The Quaker Girl*, now recreated in London with an almost frantic vigour and a pair of expressive eyebrows. With him were the deceptively casual George Grossmith, whose hands were as eloquent as Coyne's eyebrows, and Binnie Hale as Nanette. The plot depended on the fact that a business man, happily married, had highly agreeable friends at Nice, Bath, and Harrogate; he visited them in rotation. Nobody minded about the plot, and not much time had been left to consider it.

Strangely, *Nanette* had not been played in New York. When it began its 665 performances at the Palace on March 11, 1925, an American company had been acting it for forty-three weeks in Chicago, and the Broadway run did not begin until September. "I want to be happy" was not in the original American production. The authors felt that something more was needed, and this something, after an all-night session for Youmans and the lyric-writer, Irving Caesar, came out as "I want to be happy". Everyone was happy at the next performance: *Nanette* went on from there. In London Herbert Farjeon wrote: "It prances, bubbles, makes rings of joy like a dog let loose in a field; it goes with a swing and a scamper. . . . Most musical comedies attempt to fling care to the winds, but the winds blow the care back in most of their faces." James Agate added: "I should have to go back twenty years to find a match for it. The music does more than carry the gallery-boy away; it goes to the head of the dilettante as well." As *The Belle of New York* had done thirty years earlier, *Nanette* led a fashion. It went so fast that it was said Coyne and Grossmith had to be massaged between the acts; many in the audience could have done with the same attention. During the first eighteen weeks 250,000 people saw and heard *Nanette*. It ran—and for once that is the exact word—until well into 1927.

In comparison, *Rose Marie*, which began at Drury Lane not much more than a week after *Nanette*, seemed uncommonly slow. (For some reason, it struck me as even slower when they did it on ice during the ephemeral fashion of the nineteen-fifties.) But Rudolf Friml's romantic score, in an older, ampler tradition than *Nanette's*, was just as singable, and Edith Day at once took the measure of Drury Lane. The comedy, alas, was dreadful. Billy Merson, in the laborious irrelevances of the funny man—he was called Hard-Boiled Herman, and deserved it—had to rely upon his burlesque dancing, though such jokes as these would sound through Drury Lane for two years: "Why did the cat whine?"—"So would you if you had so many violin-strings inside you", and "Why do you wear those spurs?"—"Well, you never know when you may meet a horse." Luckily, there was the Totem dance for the chorus (it included Eileen Carey, who would become Mrs. Sean O'Casey, and Marjorie Robertson, later Anna Neagle). Sets for "a romance of the Canadian Rockies" were suitably massive. With the spectacle to hold the eye, and Friml's music ("Indian Love Call" and "Rose Marie") to take the ear, the production conquered: much to the grief of the ticket agencies who were too timid to risk a deal until it was too late. Sir Alfred Butt then refused their offer, so that during the two years' run of *Rose Marie* they had to pay the full price for tickets without discount.

True, facing some indifferent reviews, *Rose Marie* did totter a little before it settled to its long life. The furiously jazzed *Mercenary Mary*, which had a shorter life but a gay one in the Hippodrome, a theatre suitably garish, was in the *Nanette* mood if without the same early-in-the-morning quality; a farcical drunk scene clogged it, but it was danced with breathless vim. It had a metallic, self-conscious brightness ("common and disorderly", objected Herbert Farjeon, "with the smell of cigars all over it"), and such players as June, Peggy O'Neil, Sonnie Hale at quivering speed, and A. W. Baskcomb, despairing and perpetually distempered, whipped the night along. London responded as New York had done, and as Clayton and Waller had hoped, to "I'm a little bit fonder of you", and even to "Honey, I'm in love with you", though one critic described this as "a 'blue' of direst melancholy, accompanied by orchestral caterwaulings in comparison with which the wail of the banshee is a whoop of joy". Another critic was quite sure that what he called musical plays of "high kicking, pep and very little sentiment" would not last; that a time would arrive when an audience would not wish to stumble from a theatre, dazed by speed, to go on dancing somewhere else in the new Brighter London. "Solid, tuneful musical plays," he prophesied sternly, "will come back to their own." One "solid, tuneful" musical comedy that fared well this year was *Katja the Dancer*, with a professional Lonsdale book. It appeared at both the Gaiety and Daly's, a feat comparable to getting a First at both Oxford and Cambridge. The romance was muffled in plush, but Gene Gerrard and Ivy Tresmand would get eight or nine calls a night for their duet, "Leander", and Miss Tresmand, always a neat comedienne, had some admiring publicity because she refused to have her hair shingled. "Perhaps," she explained, "it is a touch of Samson in me." *Katja* aside (its heroine was Lilian Davies) the more orthodox musical play had poor luck.

Oscar Asche, in particular, had a discouraging year. He had been to Australia and New Zealand after *Cairo* had left His Majesty's, and he did not return until 1924, and a miserable week with a light comedy from the French at the theatre that had been his home for nearly six years. Early in 1925 the unaccountable James White of Daly's asked him to produce the musical comedy *Cleopatra*, with Evelyn Laye, and Oscar Straus music. White was a domineering, blue-eyed financial buccaneer, who at the moment had theatrical aspirations, and who was enjoying himself at Daly's more than some of his associates did. He insisted on helping to direct his own productions, with results that could be catastrophic. Asche, able to handle most people, got on with him easily enough. Even so, White had to be told that when an actor held up three small leather bags, proclaiming "Each bag contains a million gold pieces", the poor fellow was bearing in his arms twenty-one tons dead-weight. "Punctilious, aren't you?" said White to Asche. "But we'll get over that. We'll make it notes." *Cleopatra*, spectacular

86. Alice Nikitina and Serge Lifar in the
Balanchine ballet, *La Chatte*, in the Diag-
hilev season at the Princes Theatre, 1927.
The scenery and costumes were of talc.

87. The Victoria Girls were a permanent
feature of the Victoria Palace programme
in 1927: "Owing to the continued popu-
larity of their delightful dances, the Directors
have renewed their contract for a further
lengthy period." The troupe was trained by
Rodney Hudson.

88. Emma Haig and the chorus of *The Girl Friend* (Palace Theatre, 1927) singing and dancing
"Step on the Blues" in the garden of the Hotel Wendell in the Canadian Rockies.

89. Richard Dolman and Jessie Matthews sing an early Rodgers and Hart success, "My Heart Stood Still," in Cochran's London Pavilion revue, *One Dam Thing After Another*, 1927.

90. In full voice, the crew of H.M.S. *Inscrutable*, led by Alice Morley, rouses a seaport in China with the Negro spiritual, "Hallelujah!": a scene from *Hit the Deck*, which ran for 277 performances at the London Hippodrome in 1927.

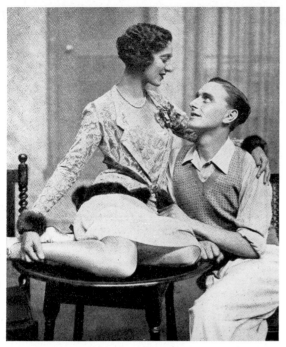

91. Gertrude Lawrence and Harold French
sing "Won't you do-do-do what you've
done-done-done before?" in Gershwin's
Oh, Kay! at His Majesty's Theatre, 1927.

92. The Red Shadow (Harry Welchman)
woos Margot (Edith Day) in the harem:
a scene from *The Desert Song*, Theatre Royal,
Drury Lane, 1927.

93. "Biff Morton rather carried away": Laddie Cliff and the Tiller Girls in *Lady Luck*, Carlton
Theatre, 1927.

94. A provocative situation in Miles Malleson's *The Fanatics*, with Ursula Jeans and Owen Nares, Queen's Theatre, 1927.

95. *The Lady-in-Law*, Wyndham's, 1927: The barrister (Edith Evans) "returns to womanhood", watched doubtfully by Frederick Leister.

96. Ellis Jeffreys (Mrs. Wislack) and Ronald Squire (the Duke of Bristol) snowed up in the Highlands in Frederick Lonsdale's comedy, *On Approval*, which ran for 469 performances at the Fortune, 1927.

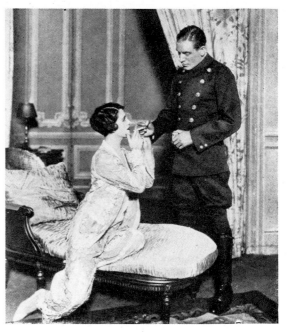

97. *Potiphar's Wife*, Globe Theatre, 1927: "The Countess of Aylesbrough (Jeanne de Casalis), casting her eye on the handsome chauffeur (Paul Cavanagh), orders him to mend the electric fan in her dressing-room late at night."

certainly, was nothing more. Evelyn Laye is unlikely to remember with any marked wistfulness her reign over Upper and Lower Egypt, a reign during which (boasted the programme) "her every action is carefully studied from tomb-paintings, from pictures written by long-dead scribes in the Books of the Dead". Clearly, this must have relieved the Egyptologists who normally formed the bulk of a Daly's audience.

Asche soon had other matters on his mind. He had written a musical play, *The Good Old Days*, which he staged at the Gaiety with his usual determined, built-up realism. He was almost the last of the "realistic spectacle" men. Several years before, when he put on *As You Like It*, he used two thousand pots of fern, large clumps of bamboo, and cartloads of autumn leaves. *The Times* had called *Chu-Chin-Chow* "fantastic, polyphonic, polychromatic Orientalism . . . a rich beauty-show, an audacious *décolletage* in both black and white, a gorgeous heap of coloured stuffs". Now, in *The Good Old Days*, with its Cecil Aldin sets, Asche used hunters, greyhounds, twelve-and-a-half couple of foxhounds, and a dun and white donkey, and he covered the stage with real courtyard cobbles, so cemented down that it took a fierce struggle to lift them when the next play was needed (after thirty-seven performances). He chose himself to play a rascally Earl. "Two years before, the Earl of Jawleyford had driven to suicide the Count of Castile, father of a strolling singer and highwayman known as the Black Spaniard, who would be impersonated by a wealthy young widow, of partly Spanish extraction, called Lady Micky Malone." Perfectly simple: it was what Asche considered to be "the full-blooded life of those days". Unluckily it met first-night rowdiness, prompted by some unemployed chorus men and girls who had a mistaken grievance. A glum business; but the play, in spite of its Percy Fletcher music, was just as glum; it came ten years too late.

The only other musical play of the year that rings at all in the memory is *Betty in Mayfair*, a version of *The Lilies of the Field* about the twin who goes tactfully Victorian when expedient. It had a better book than usual because its original dramatist, John Hastings Turner, adapted it himself, with Harold Fraser-Simson's music, and Evelyn Laye was happier and more relaxed than she had been as Cleopatra. (Hastings Turner had written the book of the Daly's failure as well.)

If there were some dreary nights in the straight theatre, plays vaulted over each other so quickly during the Twenties that failures were forgotten—

except by their backers and casts—within a few nights of collapse. The Broadway theatre had become the fashionable influence of the time; but hardly anything that came from America during 1925 has left its marks on the sand (*Dancing Mothers, Salomy Jane, Cobra, The House of Glass,* are among the litter of titles). True a version of Somerset Maugham's short story *Rain* was as relentless as its tropical downpour: 750 gallons fell at each performance. Tallulah Bankhead, on hearing that Maugham did not want her to have the coveted part of the prostitute Sadie Thompson, had hysterics outside Basil Dean's office at the St. Martin's, and "fled down the stairs, sobbing". A murky little affair called *Tarnish* (the kind of title the Gay Twenties loved) was just being transferred. Dean had suggested that Miss Bankhead might like to take over another prostitute in this, but he gathered after a moment or so that she was not interested. *Tarnish,* designed to show what a life crowded with incident one might have in New York on a New Year's Eve, at least allowed Olga Lindo—who was the chosen Sadie Thompson—Nora Swinburne, and that splendid young actor Francis Lister to give everything they had. "If acting could turn a feuilleton into *belles lettres,* these three would have done it," said Agate.

The only important American play (if we omit *Sun Up,* hickory-tough, with a mother to match, acted by Lucille La Verne) was Eugene O'Neill's *The Emperor Jones.* On a West Indian island a hunted Negro dictator fled for his life among the thronging visions of the forest and the thudding, tormenting drums. Thinly acted, it could have been intolerable. Paul Robeson was genuinely a man distraught, his first arrogance fraying to the extreme of superstitious terror.

Not many serious English plays stood from the year's thronging visions. One of the most civilised and touching was J. R. Ackerley's *The Prisoners of War,* with its interned men at Mürren who lived in a closed-circle world of waiting, of agonised repression. Its acting by Robert Harris and George Hayes honoured a play of mental strife. Sutton Vane, in *Overture,* failed to do for the life before birth what he had done for the life after death. Matheson Lang, in *The Tyrant,* by Rafael Sabatini, had a flamboyant night with Cesare Borgia, Duke of Valentinois and Romagna. Galsworthy attacked the sensational Press in a fierce drama, *The Show,* that might be required reading even now for the Press Council, and has worn better than its very brief original run suggested. Michael Arlen's *The Green Hat* ("She has such clean

eyes," "I want the final ultimate decency") was a preposterous romance—
a modish word this year—into which Tallulah Bankhead, keeping her face
very straight, and acting like the loyal and gallant professional she was, went
direct from Coward's *Fallen Angels*. There appeared to be no excuse for
The Green Hat and its suicidal heroine, but fashion ordained that it must take
the stage. Was it not a best-seller? Any writer feels that he must be incom-
petent if he cannot clip and wrench his best-seller into a play. (Bear it to the
stage, his friends tell him, for it is likely, were it but put on, to prove most
royally.) And yet after the inevitable lopping and topping much of a book's
quality has disappeared. "Bless thee, thou art translated."

During 1926, in the new experimental theatre at Barnes, just over Hammersmith Bridge, Thomas Hardy's own version of *Tess of the D'Urbervilles*,
made in the mid-Nineties, reached the stage. In later years Ronald Gow
would bring *Tess* plausibly to the theatre by ignoring a vast swathe of the
novel, and opening, in mid-career, upon the wedding night. But Hardy,
three decades earlier, had no special theatrical guile. The tragedy owed a
short London run to the performance of Gwen Ffrangcon-Davies, who may
have looked Pre-Raphaelite, but who had imagined herself into Hardy's
Wessex. Ivor Brown said of her: "This Tess, so delicate as to be an elfin
figure, would never have reached the hangman's hands; farm-labour, such
as Tess endured, would have been an earlier executioner. Yet the actress
who does not look the part, manages to become the part. If there is not
the full physique of the daughter of toil, there is all the inarticulate anguish
of the stricken child of nature whose brain cannot reckon with a world so
harsh." One veteran dramatist admired her, Henry Arthur Jones, who wrote
with enthusiasm to Hardy, "I find it true to Arnold's favourite word 'fortifying'." Another of the plays in the little theatre at Barnes was less fortifying,
but it also came to the West End: Mordaunt Shairp's painful study in psy-
chology, *The Offence*, planned to show the terrors that may overtake a man
who cannot pluck from his memory some rooted sorrow of boyhood. Harcourt
Williams acted on his nerves; few could drive so surely at the very heart of
pathos, but he was seldom allowed the chance.

It remained, on the whole, a year of comedy—perhaps that should have
been its label—assuming that we can include now such puzzle-plays as
Nine Forty-Five, in which practically everyone except the author confessed to
murder; *Number Seventeen*, an English melodrama that, dangerously, mixed

too much laughter with its shocks, and allowed Leon M. Lion, as a useful merchant seaman, to give one of those complicated character-portraits that pleased him so much; and *The Ghost Train* by Arnold Ridley, who knew just what the public needed. No one in life enjoys waiting bleakly at midnight, dead of the night's high noon, in a bleaker waiting-room. Never mind: bring the scene to the theatre, and all will respond clamorously. Add a presumed spectral train, a silly-ass comedian, a huddle of assorted passengers, a station-master voluble and venerable, and a quite absurd explanation about china-clay and gun-running, and everyone will be as happy at evening's end as any train-spotter on the prow of a busy platform. No doubt *The Ghost Train*, frequently in revival somewhere, is enjoyed by connoisseurs who live near a railway and who are used to trains that pass in the night. In 1925, Arnold Ridley—who took his inspiration from Mangotsfield in Gloucestershire—reinforced the oldest truism: that an audience likes to see and hear on the stage things that, out of the theatre, it will ignore. I found myself absorbed because of a regional loyalty. The station was Fal Vale on a Cornish branch line. It was not the same when, during the nineteen-fifties, the play became a musical comedy under the name of *Happy Holiday* and was shifted to the Highlands—even if the off-stage train (drum, thunder-sheet, cylinder of compressed air, and garden roller, said Eric Maschwitz) continued to sound more like a train than anything the best railways can offer.

Ben Travers's *A Cuckoo in the Nest* also came from the West Country, from Somerset: I still hope to track Maiden Blotton on the map. The *Cuckoo* began the ordered chaos of Travers farces at the Aldwych, tanglewood tales that were among the truest comic largesse of the Twenties. The Aldwych fellowship was gloriously of its day, with the glazed eye and gusty bark of Tom Walls, the quicksilver goof of Ralph Lynn, the enormous feather boa that was Mary Brough, and Robertson Hare, sepulchral bittern, at per-secution's heart. He had not reached full martyrdom in 1925; in *A Cuckoo in the Nest* he was merely a bicycling parson, the Rev. Cathcart Sloley-Jones. This judicious comment on the current divorce laws stays with me now less for its wisdom than for the moments when Ralph Lynn fooled with a spring blind, when he laced himself into reef-knots in his uncontrollable desire to sleep under a washstand, and when Mary Brough wore the blue-black frown of the Prussian Baptist landlady of the Stag and Hunt at Maiden Blotton, whose rooms were Fully Occupied. ("If all landladies were like her, Brighton beach would be one large dormitory.") First among these, I think, the sight of Lynn, that Tenniel sketch, with his monocle-dropping, his knuckle-biting, and the gags that slightly bothered his author. In his autobiography, *Vale of Laughter*, Travers says: "I felt uneasy about taking the nominal responsibility for a line like this: when, having written a false name in the visitors' book, the entry is inspected by the puritanical landlady: 'You don't write very clear.' —'No. I've just had some very thick soup.' I gently protested, but Ralph said he'd like to try it, and it always got a big laugh. After all, it's exactly the sort of thing Ralph himself would have said in the circumstances." There is room for a monograph on gagging. It would include the First Grave-digger's line that Cedric Hardwicke heard once in Stourbridge: "But stay! I am expecting a gal on a bier."

Many leagues separated the Stag and Hunt at Maiden Blotton from *The Man With a Load of Mischief*, the inn on the Bath Road that gives its title to Ashley Dukes's Regency conversation-piece. It is a constant rebuke to the clumsy writer; a play with an ivory gloss in which the fable of a night at an inn matters far less than the manner of its telling. At this hour in the Gay Twenties, the language of the theatre was dwindling to the tic-tac of a type-writer. Ashley Dukes, dramatist and critic, who had never failed to care for dialogue of rhythm and judgment, here lit candle upon candle in the imagina-tion: the picture of the Nobleman on the country road, its "feathered elms like striding cockerels", the soliloquies in which the Man's thoughts met the silence: this was an enchantment from a time hardly prodigal in enchant-ments, and the speaking of Fay Compton, Leon Quartermaine, and Frank Cellier made of it a play to be heard.

Noël Coward, still the theatre's audacious child, cared less for the permanent effect of his dialogue than for its momentary thrust in the theatre. His plays were Stop Press news; and yet I believe that such a comedy as *Hay Fever*, written in three days, in which the to-and-fro volleying of the dialogue is at its swiftest, will endure as a period piece. It is about a not very quiet week-end in the Cookham house of a famous retired actress who acts her head off in private life. Marie Tempest played her with entranced virtuosity, though when Coward read the script to her, she had been tactless enough to doze. The diversion on the river bank of Bohemia has an irresistible final scene: the week-end guests, faint and desperate, steal off, one by one, into the morning while the Bliss family argues at its late breakfast-table about the precise topography of Paris. *Fallen Angels*, less good, was criticised for the long second act, Edna Best and Tallulah Bankhead tipsily garrulous. Coward, taking his call at the première of *Hay Fever*, murmured that at any rate the new comedy was as clean as a whistle. But the early picture of Julia and Jane, bright young things of their time, waiting for the lover who did not arrive, had been amusing in its sugared malice, its fussy watchfulness. To-day the years have not injured that know-all parlourmaid who would have sent Patience screaming from a monument. Tallulah Bankhead, learning her part in four days to replace Margaret Bannerman who left the cast during rehearsals, had one simple line, "Oh dear, rain!" On the first night, still sore from the loss of Sadie Thompson, she could not shrug off the temptation to say, "My God! *rain*!" in her Sadiest voice. The audience rose to it.

Those fallen angels would have got on with Frederick Lonsdale's people in *Spring Cleaning* and *The Last of Mrs. Cheyney*, two other plays of the year. (Tallulah Bankhead had refused both leading parts in *Spring Cleaning* in the single-minded hope that she might reach *Rain*.) It was an hour for cynicism. The Gay Twenties, now at their most metallic, had decided that it was fashionable to say in public anything that convention had forbidden, and to repeat it, if possible, three times. A biting little wind from the Restoration had cut suddenly across the decade. Dramatists, suitably invigorated, responded with work that could blend the sophisticated and the sentimental. In *Spring Cleaning*, known already in New York, and produced in London during the often dead days of January, an easy wit proved to be a trite moralist. Luckily, his audience was concerned more with the method than the moral, and Lonsdale's method was to put a high theatrical burnish on his dialogue and to let his actors do the rest. They did it. Ronald Squire, particularly, did it in *Spring Cleaning* ("With a charm of manner, there's a hell of a lot of fun to be had in cathedral towns"). Edna Best, not yet the constant nymph, wore an Eton crop and a monocle. Lonsdale's idea was simple. When a happily-married wife gets sucked into a vortex of very curious friends, and even contemplates elopement with a sleek man of the world, her husband brings a prostitute to a dinner party, and the friends, offended, vanish. The Devil had the best tunes; the husband was a dull dog, and the wicked Ernest Steele held the comedy. Prostitutes in the theatre of 1925 were thought to be madly daring. This one had an improbable habit of talking as Wilde's people talk in the dramatic toils: "She looked like a woman being stabbed with a thousand knives. You've crushed her soul into small pieces, and you're not going to find it too easy to mend again." Cathleen Nesbitt, in the plaid skirt of vice, said this sort of thing as well as any actress could, and kept the right flaunt throughout. But it could not have been easy.

Lonsdale was better when he could concentrate on epigram. This is his way in *The Last of Mrs. Cheyney*, which is possibly regarded with more respect to-day—that is, when it is regarded at all—than by the critics of 1925. None the less, it was fashion's peak: it must have been as difficult to edge into the opening performance on September 22, 1925 (Gladys Cooper and Gerald du Maurier in the cast), as, on April 30, 1958, it was difficult to get into *My Fair Lady* at Drury Lane. Notoriously, authors suffer if they have to read their plays to a star. Just as Marie Tempest dozed during *Hay Fever*, so Gerald du Maurier dozed when Lonsdale read *Mrs. Cheyney* to him at Cannon Hall, Hampstead. Infuriated, the star-crossed dramatist fled; the correct quarrel followed, and du Maurier lost the rights for Wyndham's. Instead, he produced it, and played Lord Dilling, at the St. James's: Ronald Squire, who shared the du Maurier style, the suave throw-away delivery that hid a technique of steel, was also in the cast. The first night was a tumult of cheers. Du Maurier ended it by singing in what—according to Lonsdale's daughter and biographer, Frances Donaldson—was "a not very notable tenor", the words that had been used in the first act: "I want to be happy, But I won't be happy Till I've made you happy, too." (We have heard them earlier.) On the revival of *Mrs. Cheyney*, at the Savoy in 1944, Tyrone Guthrie, its director, put it into Edwardian dress and called it "a comedy of the day before yesterday". The first flying-bomb lunged across London a few hours later: Guthrie's change was just. One act, the third, set on the loggia at breakfast, is secure in twentieth-century comedy: it is the scene that Lonsdale, almost in Sheridan's mood, re-wrote while the first and second were being rehearsed. Some of the rest has faded; but we can concede that the tale of the notorious Mrs. Cheyney—a pearl-thief, a former Clapham shopgirl masquerading as an heiress—and of the gay Lord Dilling, who would have nodded casually to Quex, has real theatrical bravura.

Four or five productions remain. First, we can notice that *Charlot's Revue* had been changing its editions monthly. Gertrude Lawrence and Beatrice Lillie, either separately (Lillie as Wanda Allova, the ballerina of "Sealed Feet"), or together, as in "Fallen Babies", beaming and sulky in their prams, knew the secrets of this brand of burlesque as intimately as any living players. In revue you cannot make, or drop, your bricks without suitable straws in the hair, and the star dressing-rooms at the Prince of Wales's were littered with them. Charles B. Cochran, after his enforced preoccupation with the Rodeo (and also after his first Trocadero cabaret), came back gallantly to the Pavilion with a Noël Coward revue, *On With the Dance*. This was the one with "Poor Little Rich Girl", two Massine ballets, Delysia, Douglas Byng, and the new Cochran Young Ladies. *Still Dancing*, by Arthur Wimperis and Ronald Jeans, followed it immediately, to less excitement, though we remember a burlesque that said the last word on *Spring Cleaning*: Gospo's dinner-table introduction of Bodega (Hermione Baddeley) to his wife Candelabra. Cochran used his Young Ladies for the Trocabaret, *Bon Ton*, as well: it was, in effect, a set of ballet divertissements. Sophie Tucker, union of sun-burst and thunderbolt, sang for many suppers in the *Playtime Revels* at the Piccadilly; Layton and Johnstone, the coloured duettists, played on and on at the Café de Paris; and the *Midnight Follies* heard the chimes at the Hotel Metropole. Nothing more was done about a plan for cabaret shows by the Thames, with dancing and mixed moonlight bathing. It must have been a forlorn hope from the first.

I cannot believe that those planners would have bothered about three of the major theatrical events of 1925: the recognition in London of Sean O'Casey and of Chekhov, and the dispute over *Hamlet* in modern dress. *Juno and the Paycock* was easily the best play of the year; it would have been in most years. Its author, Sean O'Casey, had been a Dublin labourer. *Juno*, written in 1924 and presented at the Abbey, was his second full-scale tragi-comedy of Dublin during the "troubles". Its "Captain" Jack Boyle, slow-strutting, consequential waster of the taproom; Juno, his compassionate wife; and Joxer Daly, quotation-frothing jackal, became at once indelible figures of the theatre, and in London Arthur Sinclair, Sara Allgood, and Sydney Morgan acted them with genius: nothing can cloud Sara Allgood's last tragic cry in the regality of grief, or that vision of Sinclair observing for the thousandth time that the world was in a state o'chassis. Facially and vocally, Sinclair astonished: here he would pause to cock an eye like an affronted rooster, there he would send a tiny jet of speech gurgling and frothing in a cascade, or else the voice would whirl like clapper or rattle (no one could make more of the boss-word "tatheraraa"). In O'Casey we met again the Elizabethan fusion

98. "You cur!": Leslie Crosbie (Gladys Cooper) kills Geoffrey Hammond (S. J. Warmington) in the prologue of W. Somerset Maugham's *The Letter*, Playhouse, 1927.

99. "The wedding that does not come off—and the dress that does": Toni (Tallulah Bankhead) tears off her lace wedding dress when the bridegroom repudiates her. A scene from *The Garden of Eden*, Lyric Theatre, 1927.

100. This is *The Terror*. In Edgar Wallace's Lyceum melodrama, 1927, Dennis Neilson-Terry rescues Mary Glynne from "Mr. Goodman" (Felix Aylmer). We can now safely reveal the identity of the villain.

101. "Queer—very queer!": The butler (Gordon James) in Ben Travers's *Thark*, 1927, announces to the Aldwych team that his name is Death.

of farce and black tragedy, the voice for rhetoric, for speech like a kiln newly fired. Granville-Barker described the early work as plays of "a spontaneous realism". They have a design so bold that the Bankside men would have greeted O'Casey as a brother; but I have lost my first desire to call the plays realistic. Potential Paycocks and Joxers doubtless abounded in Dublin during the years of "chassis", and possibly abound yet; but I am not confident that any of them would have spoken with the royal air of O'Casey.

Chekhov had taken far longer than O'Casey to become acclimatised to London. To-day he is part of the classical repertory in Britain. Before 1924 he had been known over here only for productions tentative and timid. In a world accustomed to the well-made drama, to shapeliness and formality, the silver drift of Chekhov's mind must have seemed merely careless play-writing. But 1925 was ready for him, as it was ready for so much else, and J. B. Fagan's company came down from Oxford to the Lyric, Hammersmith (again the stage's benefactor), with the masterpiece of *The Cherry Orchard*, John Gielgud as the perpetual student.

Much of the play is extraordinarily amusing as well as being on the splinter-edge of tears. We stand by the death-bed of old Russia. The orchard, as Stanislavsky, the first producer said, "hides in itself and all of its flowering whiteness the great poetry of the dying life of aristocracy." London yielded to *The Cherry Orchard's* sweet grief, though one or two critics still jibbed, and Henry Arthur Jones, enraged, said that the play was to him "the impression of someone who had entered a lunatic asylum and taken down everything the lunatics said". No matter; Chekhov had come to stay, and that autumn *The Seagull*, with Valerie Taylor as Nina, and Gielgud's Constantin, was also in the West End (whither *The Cherry Orchard* had been transferred earlier). *The Seagull*, with its ecstasies and rash-embraced despairs, is now as familiar as any of Chekhov's work; like the others, it holds autumn in its eyes.

Nanette to Chekhov: "I want to be happy" to Nina and Masha: here is a state o'chassis. Let Shakespeare end the year's record. John Barrymore had brought his nobly conceived *Hamlet* to the Haymarket Theatre during the spring. The première was a fantastic success; but all Barrymore remembered, years later, was dust and ashes: "I waited until the theatre had become dark and empty. Then I walked out on the stage, stood there, alone, looking towards the black vacuum of pit and stalls, and knew what the Viscount St. Albans meant when he said that the poets had made Fame a monster. Then

F

I went to my house in Cheyne Walk, found a bottle of beer, and decided there and then that I would quit the theatre as soon as I could do so. I might have quit it the same night, had it not been for the sake of Winston Churchill. He was so fond of our family, such a great friend, that I didn't want to let him down. A note from him next day brightened matters. . . ."

That was an important *Hamlet*; but London would talk more of *Hamlet* in Modern Dress which Sir Barry Jackson put on during his season at the Kingsway. A few days later Sir Barry, as serene as ever, was examining a set of notices that varied between "An opening out of fresh light upon the play" (*The Times*) and "The production seemed to me to be almost denuded of beauty" (*The Daily News*). Birmingham had had the modern-dress *Cymbeline* two years before, but that ruffled only the calm airs of Station Street. To face London with *Hamlet*, of all plays, was to demand trouble. The company got it; but it got astonished cheers as well. If the verse suffered, the characters stood from the text with a new force: Colin Keith-Johnston's Hamlet in plus-fours (it became the year's most maddening catch-phrase), the Polonius of Bromley Davenport, bearded and frock-coated, Frank Vosper's handsome, dangerous King, Cedric Hardwicke's Gravedigger in a bowler hat. (Interviewed before the production, he had said, as a joke, that he would be the first "sober Gravedigger": a reference to the old theatre tradition that as the actor did not come on until ten o'clock or so, it was hard for him to be sober when he did. Next day it was stated solemnly that Hardwicke would present a sober Gravedigger for the first time.)

The experiment succeeded. *Hamlet* ran from mid-August until November; people ceased to mock at eccentricity, a slick way of making Shakespeare bearable; and more writers recalled, belatedly, that until Kemble tried out his idea of a Roman toga, Shakespeare had been acted in the dress of the day or in a vague masque costume. I wonder what the Gay Twenties would have said of Tyrone Guthrie's production of *Troilus and Cressida* in 1956. Then the long contention between frivolous Troy and factious Greece was turned into a struggle between (let us say) Ruritania and the Central European Powers of the year 1912. The curtain of the Old Vic rose upon an epicene exquisite, straight from a Maugham comedy and just back from a Trojan idea of Ascot, in talk with a young man whose mirror-winking breastplate seemed to have been worn on a ceremonial parade. More alarming still, heaven-born Helen, at the grand piano in her boudoir, might have dropped in from Daly's.

VIII

1926

In the last paragraph shone the name of Ruritania. Just before Christmas 1925, in an obscure North Country Hippodrome, a play whose name does not matter now was put on by a company ruthlessly out of touch with the new day, caring nothing for speed or rebellion or experiment or youth or the Charleston, for man-of-the-world cynicism and self-conscious candour, for *Green Hats* and *Spring Cleanings*, for Čapek and Toller, for Broadway and the Stage Society. True, about the same time, a drama at the Elephant and Castle Theatre had ended richly when Lady Violet, having been lured upon the yacht, was saved by her M.P. husband. With the luck that M.P.s have, he knew a man in charge of a military airship cruising in the neighbourhood. The rest was obvious. Very proper; but my heart was with the provincial play. It was set after a war between Caronia and Moritz. Let me snatch from a treasured synopsis:

> The Prince Regent of Moritz recognises Conrad as the son that his faithless wife had carried away thirty years previously. Meantime, Prince Boris, overcome by his passion for Morini, abducts her and takes her to an old château in the woods. Lieutenant Victor disguises himself as an old housekeeper. . . .
>
> The Baroness von Schöber confesses to the Regent her part in the abduction of Conrad. . . .
>
> Beating Prince Boris to his knee, Conrad refuses to take his life and returns his sword. Prince Boris is stripped of his decorations and banished from Moritz.

There, surely, was an anachronism at the core of the Gay Twenties. Ruritania had become a blank on the map, though in the mind we could see that majestic tapestry, emerald and cobalt, crimson lake and puce, and elaborately hachured, the inner-Balkans of the theatre, a cartographer's headache with "more lines than in the new map with the augmentation of the Indies". Here were the thrones, princedoms, powers, that used to blaze in the English theatre. Once we used to know the terrain like a book, every pine-forest, every crag-piled castle, every flash of uniform: "A lover's professions, when uttered in Hessians, are eloquent everywhere." Ruritania was, of course, the living centre of this cluster of kingdoms, mountainous and shaggy-wooded, inhabited by Duchesses, scheming Prime Ministers, loyal old Generals, designing Barons, and here and there—for the look of the thing—a peasant or so. More candles burned to the square inch in those midnight ballrooms than anywhere in Europe. Even the wolves had a lustier howl.

The stage had seemed oddly bleak since a curtain had slid down upon the Balkan states, Styria, Cadonia, Novia, Kravonia, Croabia, Caronia, a dozen others, all sounding like small Atlantic liners and huddled together on the map, gorgeous birds in a storm. Musical comedy was not enough. We mourned for Hope and glory; for the Captain of Hussars, in cherry-coloured cloak, who flashed defiance at a Colonel of Cuirassiers, thigh-booted, silver-spurred; and for Princess Marietta, disguised as the prison chaplain, who saved her lover from execution at the twelfth hour. The Prince Regent of Moritz, the Baroness von Schöber—where were they? Islanded in a country Hippodrome, and not a soul to aid.

Tragic indeed; and yet, on the night of August 14, 1926, when a queue that had formed early on a blistering noon entered the pit of the St. Martin's Theatre, it found that Noël Coward, of all people, was on a journey to Ruritania. His play was *The Queen Was in the Parlour*, originally christened *Souvenir*, and then *Nadya*. It began in Paris; later it laughed for a minute, and affec-tionately, at the names of Colonel Sapt and Rupert of Hentzau. But there would be no mockery here: the play, in essence, was as much a romantic melodrama as any by Anthony Hope. Coward had written it four years earlier; it was pre-*Vortex*—though critics did not realise this—and, morning by spring morning, propped against a tombstone in the Kentish churchyard of St. Mary-in-the-Marsh, near Dymchurch, he had enjoyed the creation of Nadya, Queen of Kraja, and Prince Keri of Zalgar. The result, as it came to the St. Martin's in the summer of 1926, took the audience in the old love-or-duty manner. All present were subjects of Madge Titheradge: none could have addressed an angry crowd with more regal resolution. "The play," Coward wrote years later, "will be old-fashioned long before *The Prisoner of Zenda* and *Rupert of Hentzau*. However, I didn't make a bad job of it." That is understatement. It is strange to think that Coward should have been one of our last Ruritanians. In the legitimate theatre the Balkan map has been furled in a corner. Jean Cocteau did seek to unroll it, and to found a new kingdom in *The Eagle Has Two Heads*, but his remote country and its Queen, intolerably loquacious, soon perished in the dark.

It was Coward's most wistful year. If *The Queen* had revived Ruritania, *Easy Virtue* revived the drawing-room histrionics of Pinero and Jones. It was, in fact, a Pinerotic pastiche. Its author was fortunate to have the American actress Jane Cowl as Larita, a woman with a past, a theatrical personage given to hurling books at a statuette of the Venus de Milo, and to making third-act entries down the grand staircase, carrying a scarlet ostrich-feather fan and wearing a low-cut white gown. Impressive; but Coward was happier in the deep Balkans.

The theatre of 1926 was in a dizzy spin. (It had to meet a crippling General Strike, and that sent it spinning even more wildly.) At one minute it was as shocking as Larita; at another it was being hopefully romantic. Drama critics, in whirl with the theatre, would pass, brow-mopping, from idyllic comedy to atmospheric melodrama, from costume prattle to Broadway raffishness, from the leer to the giggle, from the foolishly brash to the richly idiotic.

Superficially, there have been various years like this much nearer to our own; but a playgoer who survived 1926 had uncommonly little idea at the end of it whither the theatre was heading, if it was heading anywhere. He would have been cast up on the granite of Lundy; Galsworthy would have inquired what he would do if he met an escaped convict; Eden Phillpotts would have invited him to a tea-party; Ben Travers would have introduced him to Gerald Popkiss, Mrs. Leverett, Harold Twine, and Admiral Juddy; he would have seen Lewis Dodd with Tessa, the constant nymph; Aloma of the South Seas would have crooned to him in the third person; he would have been carried to the eighteenth and seventeenth centuries, and to the Middle Ages; he would have dog-eared his programme, hoping for a glossary of American slang; he would have sat, politely bewildered, at a revival of *Romance*; and he would have watched, at the Coliseum, the dancing of Anton

Dolin and Phyllis Bedells—perhaps, too, the dancing of "Lola Menzeli, hailed, not without reason, as a successor to Genée". In his ears would have sounded the smoky huskiness of Tallulah Bankhead (and the gallery-cry, "Tallulah, you're wonderful!"), the sable velvet tones of Mrs. Patrick Campbell, the lost-child pathos of Edna Best, the gurgle of Yvonne Arnaud, the "great bell swinging in a dome" that was Henry Ainley, the rasp of Franklin Dyall, the sunlight-flicking cheerfulness of Jack Buchanan, and the foaming, frothing gush of spilled porter that was the voice of Maire O'Neill's Mrs. Gogan. Before him would have whisked a thatched cottage on a Devon beach, a foggy afternoon on Dartmoor, Harry Tate's moustache in alarmed swivel, the cruder pomps of old Heidelberg ("Red and Yellow! Primary colours!" he would have moaned with Lady Jane), the less conscious grandeur of an East End police station, the wig and flageolet of Samuel Pepys, and the beautiful serenity of Valerie Taylor as Our Lady, risen from an illuminated missal of the Middle Ages.

The fantastic year yielded one play that would live: Sean O'Casey's *The Plough and the Stars*, a copious and, at the last, a fiercely poignant tragi-comedy of Dublin in 1915–1916: at heart a sympathetic picture of a disrupted people, though rioters at the Abbey in February, 1926, held that it defamed the men of Easter Week. Upon the fifth night W. B. Yeats came on the stage to still the house with his scornful question: "Is this going to be a recurring celebration of Irish genius? Synge first, and then O'Casey. Dublin has once more rocked the cradle of a reputation. From such a scene in this theatre went forth the fame of Synge. Equally the fame of O'Casey is born here to-night. This is apotheosis." There was no riot in London, only scalding admiration for a piece that, in the manner of *Juno*, fused farce and stern tragedy: the farce of Fluther Good, the carpenter, and Mrs. Gogan and the Covey, and the last bitter doom, the moment when, ironically, above the fire and grief of Easter Week, rises the soldiers' chorus, "Keep the Home Fires Burning".

Certain lesser plays stood from the ruck, though no dramatist had the inspired incendiarism of O'Casey, who could fire a theatre like a torch in brushwood. In *Escape* John Galsworthy put himself in the position of a convict on a desperate break from Dartmoor. The play was ribbon-building, some of its episodes urgent and closely-written, some slack. It had, in any event, to be special pleading because the convict was a man of charm who had been convicted falsely. Moreover, Nicholas Hannen acted him; and most people in an Ambassadors' audience would have taken Hannen to their heart and their home without further question. As it was, we knew that he must be caught in the last episode, and Galsworthy brought down the curtain on the vestry of a village church: Matt Denant's "It's one's decent *self* one can't escape", the Parson's low "God keep you!", and the ringing of the church bell.

Clemence Dane's *Granite* at the same theatre, the Ambassadors, earlier in the year, had also a West Country setting. Its period, the Regency, would have astonished Ashley Dukes's Lady, Nobleman, and Man. *Granite* was as rough as its name. Without verbal decoration the dramatist spoke right on. Her play, in its fashion extended Grand Guignol, with Sybil Thorndike in relishing force, might have thrust most strongly at those who knew the outline of Lundy's iron cliffs smudged on the western horizon. Judith, the farmer's wife weary of her husband, had vowed to sell her soul to God or Devil for a month of summer with her brother-in-law, "whatever Hell you send me to." There was a laugh; in a gust of storm the Man appeared, an escaped convict —nothing like Galsworthy's—cast upon Lundy shore. Thenceforward Clemence Dane battered us against the granite, scene by scene, until Judith, helplessly alone with the stranger who had taken her in this island desolation, gave her last cry: "I know what you are now. You are the evil one. I prayed for you to come, and out of my own heart you came—the devil came."

THE MAN: Devil? Devil a bit! I wanted what I wanted, like you. And you gave me my chance to get 'em—a farm and a woman. Come here! (*He puts a hand on her shoulder. Terrified, she strives to fend him off.*) It's no use your fighting me. I'm stronger than you.

(*The curtain falls.*)

It is a drama that can still rise from the text. Capriciously, the Gay Twenties neglected it; but it might yet be reborn. Playgoers in 1926 had simpler fun with *Yellow Sands*—again the West Country—which Eden Phillpotts wrote with his daughter Adelaide. It lasted for 610 performances at the Haymarket, a mere flash-in-the-pan according to Sloane Square standards, but useful. Once more characters and dialogue outmatched plot. The scene, a fishing village with a Paul Shelving thatched cottage, and within sight of Start Point, was based presumably on Hallsands. In her will, an old woman with property to bestow, ordains—the word is true Phillpotts—that it shall go to her anti-Capitalist nephew, a bit of Red Devon. Frank Vosper, himself of Devon ancestry, knew all about this Joe Varwell (just as he had known about the King in the modern-dress *Hamlet*), but the play's lantern at the mast was Cedric Hardwicke's Uncle Dick, with his drooping grey moustache, straggle of hair, rubious nose, sucked-in cheeks, quick shamble, darting glances, and hands in pockets. Tumbledown Dick, blend of pointer and sheepdog, was a comfortably sententious lounger who had tested every public-house in the county. Hardwicke estimated that during the run he must have consumed eighty gallons of ginger ale diluted with water and called champagne, and coloured water with burnt sugar, alleged to be either sherry or port. He dressed (the oddest place for Uncle Dick) in the blue boudoir that Fay Compton had used when she was the Haymarket's leading lady. Eden Phillpotts, resolutely retiring as always, never saw the play, one that various shrewd judges preferred to *The Farmer's Wife*. Its treatment of Devon speech reaffirmed that rustic-comedy writing does not depend upon a rush to the head of dialect words, tooth-gritting plum-stones, but on the run, the rhythm of a sentence, and the idiosyncratic "curl" of a phrase.

This was very much home ground. The year also threw up several efficient and ephemeral little plays from America: comedies with such titles as *Is Zat So?* and *The Fall Guy*, to which London audiences listened dutifully (for American slang was modish); lurid dramas, such as *Broadway*, all bootleggers, show-girls, and "sex challenge" (as Thirza Tapper would have put it), which went on showing how tough it was, and to-day looks silly; and a compound of mush and violence known as *Aloma of the South Seas*: withered hibiscus, sprawl of beachcombers, tired and tarnished moon, melting milkchocolate, and a very capable actress, Vivienne Osborne. Francis Lister, even in this rubbish, was an actor unconquerably good.

Tallulah Bankhead by now was the toast of the town. "She is Medusa," said Cecil Beaton, "very exotic, with a glorious skull, high pumice-stone cheekbones, and a broad brow." In a strident comedy, *The Gold Diggers*, she had to battle all the way through an anecdote of a chorus-girl who (said a critic) "behaves outrageously, dances a daring Charleston, commands every extravagance, and pretends to get drunk". Tedious; but she took one of her few important chances in England as the heroine of Sidney Howard's *They Knew What They Wanted*, a sad example of an unalluring title. She was a City waitress beguiled into marriage by an ageing Italian vine-grower in California.

102. "Help me hence, ho!": Mary Merrall (Lady Macbeth) and Eric Maturin (Macbeth), with Donalbain (Ivan Brandt) and Malcolm (Laurence Olivier), after the murder of Duncan, in the modern-dress production at the Court Theatre, 1928. *The Times* said: "We remained so conscious of anachronism that the play was not illuminated but overwhelmed."

103. Elmer Rice's expressionist drama, *The Adding Machine*, Court Theatre, 1928: Mr. Zero's own corner of Hell is an office where, as in his lifetime, he casts up figures on an infernal adding machine. With Zero (Frank J. Randell) are Joe (Robert Lang) and Lieutenant Charles (Percy Rhodes) who explain to him that it is a "cosmic laundry" where souls are washed before returning to earth.

104. Ursula Jeans, Noël Coward, and Raymond Massey in S. N. Behrman's comedy, *The Second Man*, Playhouse, 1928.

105. The surprise of the season: Gracie Fields appears with Gerald du Maurier in the drama, *S.O.S.*, at the St. James's, 1928.

106. "Young Woodley goaded to desperation": David Horne, Jack Hawkins, Frank Lawton (Woodley), Henry Mollison, and Derrick de Marney in John van Druten's play, Savoy Theatre, 1928.

107. Hands Up at the Haymarket: the murder that was made to look like suicide. H. R. Hignett, Frank Cellier, and Spencer Trevor in A. A. Milne's *The Fourth Wall*, 1928.

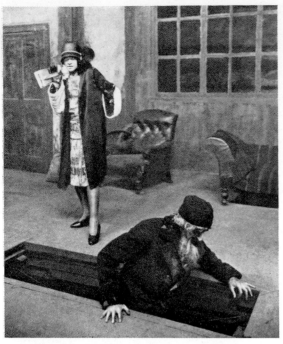

108. Down the Trap at the Lyceum: Peggy
O'Neil (Ann Pennington) sees the "ghost"
of Li Joseph (Wilfrid Caithness) in Edgar
Wallace's *The Flying Squad*, 1928.

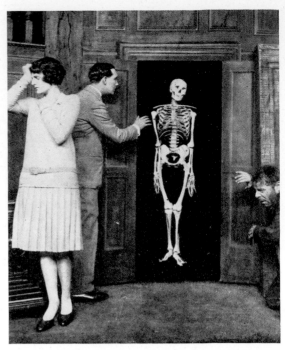

109. Skeleton at the Strand: Dr. Ziska's
lonely house in *The Monster*, 1928, also
contains a Negro without a tongue and a
man without a face. Jane Welsh, George
Relph, and Edmund Gwenn in one of the
richer melodramas.

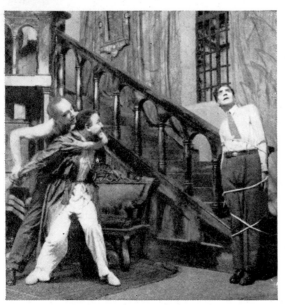

110. Sadism at the Little: Ion Swinley,
Charles Laughton, and J. H. Roberts in
A Man with Red Hair, adapted by Benn
Levy from the Hugh Walpole novel.

111. Agatha Christie's Poirot (Charles
Laughton) views the body with J. H.
Roberts in *Alibi* (Michael Morton's
version), Prince of Wales's, 1928.

Her acting, said Agate, was felt from the heart and controlled by the head. Before then, at the St. Martin's, she had a tiring experience in Sir Patrick Hastings's *Scotch Mist*. According to her own précis, she played a wild baggage, wife of a British Cabinet Minister, who was trying to lay waste all Downing Street. "Upset by its plot, the Bishop of London denounced it from his pulpit, and changed a failure into a long-run success."

Rumours had got round that in her year of many parts Tallulah Bankhead might appear as Tessa Sanger in *The Constant Nymph*, Basil Dean and Margaret Kennedy's version of Miss Kennedy's novel. It would have been the quaintest casting. What the play needed was the Edna Best waif. She was in a line of actresses that would go on to Elisabeth Bergner and the late Fifties' Dorothy Tutin: all specialists in child-pathos, though now and then the voices would fade like the Mouse's in *Alice* with the twist-and-dwindle that Carroll expressed typographically. But Edna Best, who could achieve a rare tenderness and sorrow, was born for Tessa: "She was instinct," said Herbert Farjeon, "with the dogged, passionate faith of youthful love."

Noël Coward hinted uncannily at Lewis Dodd's musical genius, though he detested the part during the month he acted it. He was playing under nervous strain, and he had to cope with a Basil Dean production in which the shifting of a knife or fork had to fit significantly into the general scheme. It was all terrifyingly complicated, but exciting, and it remained exciting when John Gielgud (who had previously understudied and played for Coward in *The Vortex*) took over Lewis Dodd, after nearly three weeks, for the rest of an eleven months' run. He remembers how Basil Dean, with an eye for the minutest naturalistic detail—and it impressed any audience, whatever the company felt—rehearsed the musical party over and over again "until the guests nearly went mad, making bright conversation in high-pitched voices, and stopping short with abrupt resignation every few minutes, when the same person made the same mistake for the eighth time and the whole scene had to be done all over again". The result was worth the toil, for *The Constant Nymph* is one of the constant memories of its period.

During its run, *The Ringer*, at Wyndham's across the courtyard, was establishing Edgar Wallace in the theatre. Soon (the cynics said) he would be writing a new play every other week-end. He had tried, often and unluckily, to capture the stage, and now with the aid of du Maurier's production —and helpful revision—he had managed it at last. He was able in a very short time to evolve a convoluted plot, and he had, too, a millrace of Cockney humour. It was a relief after the grittier type of clue-docketing thriller that had to be worked out on squared graph-sheets, or the Broadway rattle-traps, panel-plays, that had no possible basis in human behaviour. The surprise in *The Ringer* was a real surprise. Most people (after thirty years it is a secret no longer) were startled when the old Scottish police-doctor was revealed as a master-crook. Leslie Faber—for whom every part was a character-part: he never stood lazily outside them—played this crusty Lomond, and on his first appearance, early in the night, wore a very heavy make-up. Once this had been fixed in the mind, he removed the make-up bit by bit, scene by scene. In the final scene very little of his "character" disguise remained, and the last change was rapid. Dorothy Dickson, in *The Ringer*, transformed herself into a straight actress as Cora Ann, and Gordon Harker was firmly of Hoxton.

For the rest, it was the year of *Rookery Nook*, with the Popkisses, Poppy Dickey, Admiral Juddy ("swearing in Chinese"), Mrs. Leverett ("I will come at eight-thirty in the morning; earlier than that I cannot be"), and the Prussian stepfather who had just turned out his daughter for eating whortle-berries against his orders: a crisis possible only at Chumpton-on-Sea, Somerset, not too far from Maiden Blotton. The girl was Winifred Shotter, thenceforth the Aldwych heroine. It was the year of *Berkeley Square*, with its tingling experiment in time and its lost lovers. It was the year of *The Marvellous History of St. Bernard* and of Valerie Taylor as the Queen of Heaven who looked, said Hubert Griffith, like Botticelli's Madonna of the Magnificat. It was the year in which Edith Evans, in an Anglicised and modernised *Rosmersholm*, a Rebecca in an almond-green jumper suit, and with her hair waved and shingled, projected that secret woman with an intensity (said Ivor Brown) that shrivelled the attempted naturalism of the revival. And it was the year in which Mrs. Patrick Campbell appeared as the Countess Strong-i'-th'-Arm in an extravaganza of the new-poor, *What Might Happen*, by H. F. Maltby. It might have been a thoroughly comic evening (Lilian Braithwaite was in the cast), but Mrs. Campbell could not be bothered. "She sulked," wrote Maltby, "lost all interest in the production, and made no attempt to learn her lines. All she would say was: 'Oh, what a bad girl I am, aren't I? I really must learn them.'"

The theatre lists were quite unpredictable. "Everything," said a critic, "seems to be in a state of flux, or dependent upon whims, caprices, and the

capacity of individual magnates or syndicates for making profitable deals."
This uncertainty has annoyed playgoers who like to put their faith in one
theatre as they do in one newspaper, one politician, or one brand of soap.
It is only a few years since a member said seriously at a literary club debate:
"If we want a light and entertaining evening at the play, we go as a rule to
the X Theatre. I recommend it to you. We have been well satisfied at the
X for many years." It would have been discourteous and discouraging to
have observed that the play on at that moment was a limp melodrama about
a dope addict, and that for a long time the proportion of "light and entertaining
plays" had been very small. I find that this theatre, during 1926, staged *Summer
Lightning*, a revival of *The Man From Toronto*, *The Rescue Party*, *A Man Unknown*,
Virginia's Husband, *After Dark*, and *Half a Loaf*: names of plays that wavered for
a moment—summer lightning after dark—and slipped off into the night.

One theatre that held steadily to its task—Shakespeare, and opera in
English—was the Old Vic. There, during the spring, Edith Evans, in search
of fresh experience and finding it, "flashed, loomed, and laughed with divers
hues in one". She had gone to the Vic in the previous autumn. Her work,
with the fine Shakespearian Baliol Holloway, taut, spare, greyhound of a man,
as her associate, would be permanently honoured. In the West End there had
been only two major revivals. Sybil Thorndike did more with the over-valued
part of Lady Macbeth than most actresses had done. Henry Ainley's Macbeth
was uncertain: a critic called it soft-centred. Earlier in the year he had been
much better cast as Benedick, with Madge Titheradge (not yet Queen of
Kraja) as Beatrice. This *Much Ado About Nothing*, watched on the first night
by Ellen Terry, was directed by W. Bridges-Adams, from Stratford-upon-
Avon. Soon he would lose his own theatre. On a buffeting afternoon of early
March the fire alarms sounded in Stratford. It was too late. Already the old
theatre blazed, and when the fire, never explained, spread to the roof, the
March wind acted as a gigantic fan. By nightfall the first Shakespeare
Memorial lay in ruin, a mass of twisted girders and smoke-blackened bricks
among which points of flame flickered still. It would be the beginning of a
new Stratford. John Drinkwater wrote an Appeal poem, read from sixty
stages throughout England: "'Tis ours to give The life he gave us means
whereby to live." Bridges-Adams, fitting his productions cunningly to the
newest nutshell, transferred the spring festival to the stage of a cinema, and
Stratford Shakespeare went forward indomitably.

"Shall we hear this music?" asks Don Pedro of Arragon. There was music enough, of a kind, in the West End during the year, though nothing would last as *No, No, Nanette* had done. In *Princess Charming*, on *Nanette's* stage at the Palace, musical-comedy Ruritania had one of its last spectacular nights. (Novello's *King's Rhapsody* was many years in the future.) To-day *Princess Charming* means the Albert Szirmai score, and the singing of "Swords and Sabres" by John Clarke and a vociferous male chorus. George Grossmith acted King Christian II of Sylvania as if he had been vigorously starched; W. H. Berry loitered round the Court as Albert Chuff, agent for the Colossal Assurance Company; and Alice Delysia and Winnie Melville, adventuress and heroine, offered the correct duel of angels. *Princess Charming* was thoroughly efficient: the kind of musical play unlikely to be forgotten while an amateur company has a dozen or so stout hearts, lusty voices, and uniforms of emerald and old rose. Ruritania may have crumbled. Not so its marching songs—for, let us say, a Colonel of the Green Hussars and chorus:

> When this dear land's in danger
> I draw my shining blade—
> And woe unto the stranger,
> For Death's a soldier's trade:
> And the men who stay behind—
> *Pom-pom!*—
> Can thank their lucky stars
> That our foemen still must find—
> *Pom-pom!*—
> The Galloping Green Hussars.

Amateur companies still revive *The Student Prince* ("Deep in My Heart, Dear"), that brassy version of *Old Heidelberg*, which came to His Majesty's in 1926 with—said Agate—"a sunset of such brilliance that it illuminated not only the sentimental old doctor, but the occupants of the boxes on the O.P. side. A very remarkable sunset altogether, since it appeared to take place in the bar parlour of the inn".

The newer fashions had full play. The Astaires flickered through *Lady, Be Good*. Jack Buchanan and Binnie Hale were in *Sunny* (music by Kern; Claude Hulbert as Harold Harcourt Wendell-Wendell). Joseph Coyne, beaming, and A. W. Baskcomb, miserable, had their game of poker in *Queen High*.

Lupino Lane singing "I Don't Care" and "Mad", and tossing himself about the stage in a whirl of acrobatic dancing, was the salvation of a musical farce, *Turned Up* (which included the Dodge Twins). Ivy Tresmand sang "It's Nicer to be Naughty" and "Day Dreams" in *Yvonne* at Daly's. And in *Lido Lady* Phyllis Dare, gentle and gracious; Cicely Courtneidge, with her upward-flickering voice and quenchless gusto, as a film star nobody recognised; and Jack Hulbert, a dancing lighthouse, managed to bring some success to the Gaiety which just then was desperately in need of it. It was business as usual at the Winter Garden, where Leslie Henson (and he would have liked the word) as the eponymous Kid Boots, led a company that ended with the Misses Brassie, Cleek, Driver, Mashie, Fairway, Foursome, Hazard, and Green.

Cochran, at the Pavilion, had his *1926 Revue*, with Massine ballets and the tiny, shimmering French soubrette, Spinelly, who had to be carefully soothed and coaxed through her temperamental flurries. No need for this with Florence Mills: later in the year, when *Blackbirds* re-entered London, she performed her old miracle of walking on the stage and holding an audience breathless with adoration before she began to sing—"Silver Rose", perhaps, "Mandy, Make Up Your Mind", or "I'm a Little Black Bird Looking for a Blue Bird". All of this was in the pattern of the Gay Twenties. Less so *Riverside Nights*, at the Lyric, Hammersmith, where that high master of theatrical taste, Nigel Playfair, produced a revue based on the idea that no one would tremble at the names of Wordsworth, Arne, Landor, and Chekhov. No one did—though the Landor "conversation" was a mistake, soon withdrawn—but the work of A. P. Herbert, then at his satirical meridian, would have won easily on a popular vote. Here he addressed to Chekhov a few words called *Love Lies Bleeding; or, The Puss in Russian Boots*, from which we remember Miles Malleson's pessimistic newsvendor Hezekiah Topley, and James Whale as Thomas William Love, the goalkeeper who had shot the wrong man. (Leslie Mitchell had this part when *Riverside Nights* went briefly to the Ambassadors: at Hammersmith room had to be made periodically for *The Beggar's Opera*.) The very young Lyon Playfair's drama, *Lambert Simnel and Perkin Warbeck in the Reign of King Henry VII*, would have warmed the hearts of the authors of *1066 And All That*, still many years ahead: its cast included "two citizens of Yorkshire" called Mr. de Rock and Mr. de Roll. Very much lingers from this revue: Penelope Spencer performing that stately Funeral Dance for the Death of a Rich Aunt, and Dorice Fordred as the scullerymaid,

miserable in her attic and wishing that she were a movie star. And a picture
of Frederick Ashton's first ballet, *A Tragedy of Fashion; or, The Scarlet Scissors*
can reveal the presence of Ashton himself and of Marie Rambert. Altogether,
London's least-expected revue. "We could do with more of such refined
entertainments," breathed a courteous writer, "if the rococo element is
repressed judiciously."

Playfair was less happy when he ventured from his own well-charted world
into that of *The Midnight Follies*. "*Riverside Nights*," said the posters, "is full
of delights." But these were not the delights required for a supper entertainment that Sir Francis Towle, an admirer of the revue, had asked Playfair to
undertake. Here a producer could not count upon the informed and respon-
sive audience at Hammersmith. Metropole patrons wanted nothing but some
gentle and unexacting entertainment in the middle distance. In Playfair's
"review" they could not concentrate upon the stylised dancing of Penelope
Spencer and the singing of Elsa Lanchester, and they did not listen to the
lyrics of A. P. Herbert. The one number that everybody enjoyed was Norman
Griffin's "Don't Tell My Mother I'm Living in Sin". Otherwise, it appeared
that for its intended audience Nigel Playfair had insufficiently repressed "the
rococo element". As a writer on cabaret said sadly: "Though many of the
items were of great originality and interest, the whole production lacked life,
and showed a highbrow tendency which patrons did not appreciate." The
regular chorus of *The Midnight Follies* was sulky about the business, and all was
gloom until Laddie Cliff came in to pull things together by turning "review"
to "revue", getting the orchestra back to its accustomed jazzing, and allowing
such cabaret tradition as there was to guide him. Clearly, the *Follies* would
have been gayer if *The Co-Optimists* had taken charge. At various times this
year, the eleventh and twelfth programmes at His Majesty's had Gilbert
Childs as the rich man who drove by in his carriage and pair; also a Roman
sketch described curtly: Scene 1, The Roman Empire (Exterior); Scene 2,
Let's Go to Lions (Interior); Scene 3, Nero's (Extension to 2 a.m.).

In other London cabarets—extension to 2 a.m.—business was as usual:
a miniature circus ring at the Piccadilly; and the Cochran inventions at the
Trocadero, *Supper Time* (with its dancing by the Dodge Twins and by Trixie
Andrée and Jack Curtis), and, later, *Merry Go Round*, with the Young Ladies
in accustomed dignity. "London cabaret entertainments," a writer proclaimed with pride, "include every type of act, down to an educated horse."

It was a pity that Playfair did not try again; but he was always a man on his own.

There were other individualists in the theatre. Playgoers looked to the experimental outer-circle ventures at Barnes and, more prolific but less adventurous, at Kew Bridge (the "Q", shaped, like Hampstead's Everyman, from a former drill-hall). By now, too, in the West End, there must have been a dozen Sunday-night producing societies of merit. This year, at Barnes, Philip Ridgeway put on Komisarjevsky's production of another Chekhov, *Uncle Vanya*, which moved before long to the Duke of York's. Sean O'Casey, over from Dublin for the first time, went to *Vanya* with his manager, J. B. Fagan. He found himself concealed so carefully at the back of a box—a lion not yet on exhibition—that, as he wrote later in his third-person style, "The first London play he had seen he hadn't seen at all."

Perversely, no doubt, I end the record of 1926 with a play that London could hold it hadn't seen at all: James Elroy Flecker's *Don Juan*, slipped on for a Sunday night at the Court by the Three Hundred Club, with Robert Holmes as Juan, and Jean Forbes-Robertson (who had been in *Uncle Vanya*) as Lady Anna. This was Flecker's first work for the theatre—the "gorgeous play" he had conceived in a Cotswold sanatorium during the winter of 1910. Within three months *Don Juan*, worked at with passionate eagerness, was finished: Flecker wrote much of it, including the epithalamium ("Smile then, children, hand in hand") in Paris, in a room above the noise of the Avenue Wagram. It was revised during his summer honeymoon in Corfu. Before then Bernard Shaw had read it and praised it generously.

Don Juan, never acted for a West End run, reaches the stage in glistening shreds. It has a queer tremor of expectancy. We seem always to be on the edge of revelation: sun over the crest, sail above the horizon, a world behind the opening door. Several familiar poems, usually found detached, are part of the fabric of *Don Juan*; when they are spoken the stage flashes to light. The play's politics are fatal to the poet—as politics must be—but this is work to be heard not for its doctrine, but its music: "Where the fleet of stars is anchored and the young star-captains glow." Flecker was one of the young star-captains. It was sad that he should have come at last to the theatre in a decade so out of sympathy with him.

IX

1927

One night in the autumn of 1927 a provincial manager spoke to me during the second interval of a Sensational Attraction. The curtain had fallen, if I remember, on the sight of a more than commonly insipid heroine bound and gagged in a chair over a trapdoor. The hero, threatened by several revolvers, fumed in a corner, and somebody's body lay well down-stage. As a very young drama critic indeed, this seemed good enough to me, though I could not imagine at that moment how the hero would get clear. He knew nobody in charge of a military airship, and it was obviously no time for single combat with Prince Boris. Possibly he would use the resource of a serial writer with an unfailing phrase for any new instalment: "One bound, and our hero was free." While I pondered, the manager whispered to me, without the slightest hint of irony, "Won't do. Won't do. Not enough incident."

He was probably right; but I think that if he were now remembering the drama of 1927, his lost world would be very different from mine. Let me begin by saying what the year means to me before I add the events that have hardened into permanent record.

For me, then, it is the year in which du Maurier, at the St. James's, had that elaborate silent scene in Roland Pertwee and Harold Dearden's *Interference*. He played a famous specialist who suspected his wife of murder. Circumstantially, everything looked like it. Thus it must be manipulated to resemble suicide, and for exactly eight minutes du Maurier held the stage without uttering a word, as slowly, anxiously, he transformed the littered room, considering this piece of evidence and that, and turning them to new use. It might have been a tedious scene—my manager would have mourned its lack of incident—but we saw du Maurier's mind working: every action had the logic of a move in chess. The rest of the night has slipped from memory except the quiet, wry fascination, the huskiness, and the melancholy half-

112. *That's a Good Girl*, London Hippodrome, 1928: Joy the detective (Elsie
Randolph), disguised as the Dutch post-
girl, Wilhelmina, with Bill (Jack Buchanan).

113. "Roll Away, Clouds," sung by Uncle
Ned (Walter Richardson) and chorus of
cotton-pickers in *Virginia* at the Palace
Theatre, 1928.

114. Lauri Devine and the chorus, wearing
Benda masks, in Coward's "Dance Little
Lady" from *This Year of Grace!* at the
London Pavilion, 1928.

115. *So This Is Love* at the Winter Garden
Theatre, 1928: Madge Elliott and Cyril
Ritchard dance the "Mardi Gras".

116. "A Couple of Growers": Bobby Howes and Binnie Hale as Jim and Jill sing "One Man Girl" in *Mr. Cinders* at the Adelphi Theatre, 1929.

117. Settling the Knick-Knacks at the semi-detached villa in Harringay: Cicely Courtneidge and Jack Hulbert as Rose and Henry Carroway in *The House that Jack Built* at the Adelphi Theatre, 1929.

118. The Astaires sing "The Babbitt and the Bromide" to Leslie Henson in *Funny Face*, Princes, 1929.

smile of Herbert Marshall. Yet du Maurier, his fingers moving with a surgeon's delicacy, has not ceased to haunt that lost room, a fastidious wraith of the St. James's.

I think of Gladys Cooper in Maugham's *The Letter*, under the suspicious scrutiny of Leslie Faber; of a speech in *Dracula* (plenty of incident here), "Tell me, friend John, why do little spiders die?", that became one irreverent playgoer's party piece; of the vampire set in his earth-coffin at Carfax; of the intellectual vigour of *The Fanatics*, a debating play in which the youth of 1927 ranged itself behind Miles Malleson as articulately as the youth of 1956 behind John Osborne. I think of the end of *Marigold*, the slow descent of the Kingsway's green velvet curtain just before the presumed entrance of Queen Victoria; the roaring "To hell with Burgundy!" in *The Vagabond King*, one of the inescapable tunes ("Only a Rose" was another) of the late Twenties; the impersonation of a glum American magnate in a forgotten comedy, *The Happy Husband*, by an unforgotten actor, Charles Laughton; the pounding noise of a musical comedy, *Hit the Deck*; Arthur Sinclair's comic terror as he lay in his tenement bed and looked up at the Black-and-Tan of *The Shadow of a Gunman*; Edythe Baker, from Missouri, as she played "Birth of the Blues" on her white piano in *One Dam Thing After Another*; and Jessie Matthews, of the fringe and the china-blue eyes, singing "My Heart Stood Still".

Further, four things fantastically at variance. There was Martin-Harvey, among the last of the older romantic actors, on the stage of the Garrick Theatre—not for once in those cardboard melodramas (he was another fine actor addicted to the bad play), but reviving Maeterlinck's burgomaster of Stilemonde, Cyrille van Belle, who defies the Germans and who is condemned to be shot. Martin-Harvey presented the gentle hero with a nobility, entirely unaffected, that few contemporaries could have reached. We think of the homely man with the basket of grapes, the steady, kind eyes, and the musing voice: "Looked at from a distance, death seems like some horrible mountain, which shuts out the horizon; but, as we draw near, it dwindles and sinks away; and, when we are face to face with it, it is nothing."

The other plays? For one, *Thark*, at the Aldwych, with Ralph Lynn again like a Tenniel drawing of the Mad Hatter, Tom Walls in sportin' man-of-the-world imbecility, Mary Brough in ire unquenchable, and Robertson Hare awaiting the hounds. Tom Walls had decided that the new farce had to be about a haunted house, and Travers set the note at once by writing,

G

as the first word of *Thark*, its title: the name of the remote Norfolk manor where it would all happen. The last act, in a haunted bedroom, is the wildest memory: uncle and nephew (Walls called Benbow, Lynn called Gamble) in uneasy repose: a reporter under the bed, a duck-gun beside it, raps at the window, bangs upon the door, wind and thunder and tumult. When everything had gone as far as it could, Travers stopped the play suddenly. The reporter vanished through the window, curtains were blown across the room, blankets and quilt whirled from the bed, thunder boomed again, a great portrait fell from above the fireplace, brass candlesticks clanged to the ground, a gong was pelted furiously, and the curtain descended. It rose upon the spectacle of the entire cast gathered upon the stage; behind was an enormous tree-branch that had crashed through the window. As I said once, there would have been little there for the ballet critic who exhorted a ballerina to "lend more of a swooning *ritardando* to her *retiré*".

A richly preposterous end; but in my heart I still cherish the earlier scene with the butler, Jones, "a very sinister-looking man who walks with a measured, gliding step, slightly on his toes". "What is your name, Jones?" asked Lynn (we cannot separate Aldwych actors and their parts), and the reply, to the accompaniment of thunder and lightning, was a lugubrious "Death". Tom Walls remembered immediately a chap called Major Death, who was in the Blues, something that by no means surprised Lynn. What had this Death brought with him? The last post, of course. "I'll come after you with the sheets," he told the visiting manservant. And the curtain-line was simply, and sepulchrally, "What time would you like your call?" Travers tells us that in *Thark* Tom Walls provided a roll of thunder that would be the end of all rolls of stage thunder for all time. It was based on the discharge of two dozen cannon balls, borrowed from the Tower of London and bumped one by one down a long and solid flight of wooden stairs, with "stage hands simultaneously performing on thunder sheets for good measure".

That thunder rolls yet from the Gay Twenties. Another, and a gentler sound, is the voice of Gertrude Lawrence from *Oh, Kay!* P. G. Wodehouse and Guy Bolton wrote the book ("He's a topping bishop".—"What's that?" —"A bishop who plays golf"), and George Gershwin the music, neither of which mattered much, if at all. Gertrude Lawrence had hardly anything to act, but, with her shimmering sense of the ridiculous, nobody could have acted it better. One charade-scene, in which she appeared as parlourmaid to the bootlegger-turned-butler of John Kirby, was an intricate example of creative comedy: her very apron and cap were expressive. There were such clever people about as Harold French and the Dodge Twins; but, without Gertrude Lawrence, the piece would have been as blank, Dickensianly, as the faces of a baffled audience.

My fourth play is Lonsdale's four-character comedy, *On Approval*, acted in the hatbox of the Fortune, across from the gallery door of Drury Lane. ("The Fortune," wrote O'Casey in another context, "a little theatre directly opposite the towering, bully-like Royal Theatre in Drury Lane—Falstaff and the little page.") Until then it had seemed to be ill-christened. Lonsdale and Ronald Squire had not thought of it while they were trying, before production, to persuade various managers that *On Approval* was not merely a disagreeable piece about nothing in particular. But Tom Walls, who had taken the Fortune (on which he could keep a resolute eye from the neighbouring Aldwych), accepted the comedy, presented it at once with enviably certain faith in his own judgment, and secured a full year's run. Plays with a few characters and even with the telephone, miraculous life-preserver, can be tedious examples of false economy. Not so with Lonsdale. His slanging foursome is less funny to us now than it was when George, Duke of Bristol, Mrs. Wislack, and friends were first snowbound in Scotland; but at the Fortune Ellis Jeffreys could turn her glance to a death-ray, and Ronald Squire, as the graceless Duke who was the cream of the Bristols, had a swift appreciation of the exact shape and weight of a phrase. As a critic has written of him: "He possesses a quality very rare on the stage—the sense of enormity. He will say something unpardonable with the air of an artist achieving a master-stroke, and when he has finished saying it will relapse into the artist's condition of contented exhaustion."

It was not a year for the major play—of incident or otherwise—though in *The Constant Wife*, tepidly-received, Maugham offered, under a plausible Restoration title, a comedy of marital manœuvres on a theme that, oddly, Shaw might have liked. It had a difficult first night that began with confusion over tickets. People who had booked for the last row of stalls found that it had been merged, mistakenly, with the pit: a dividing rope had been moved forward too far and the result was chaos. The pit crowd, after queueing for hours, refused to give way. Compromise came at length when volunteers from the stalls yielded their places; for the rest of the evening the gangways were chaotically filled. That was the beginning, and the gallery did its part at the end by interrupting Fay Compton's speech of thanks: the second Maugham première (*The Circle* was the first) at which she had faced a disaffected gallery, though here there was a difference of opinion about the nature of the interruptions: these might have been friendliness mistimed. The play itself, artificial comedy in the diamond-cut-diamond mood, has never failed to remind me of Congreve's "Raillery, raillery, madam; we have no animosity. We touch off a little wit now and then, but no animosity". Even so, it was not important Maugham. Only one first-line dramatist brought to the theatre of 1927 a play that has lived untarnished: O'Casey's *The Shadow of a Gunman*, written and produced in Dublin four years before. It is the tale of a vain tenement poet, in the "troubles" of 1920, who has no objection to being thought a gunman if it will help him with the admiring Minnie. The play darkens to tragedy, to death and lament. "They tell me," said the author, "that it breaks all the rules. If characters live, and the play holds the audience, it's enough." They do live, and the play does hold the audience. In the *Gunman* Arthur Sinclair managed to resemble a blend of ferret and uncertain eagle, which took some doing.

There, then, are the plays, strange companions, that stick after thirty years: *The Shadow of a Gunman, On Approval, Thark, The Constant Wife*, one scene in *Interference*, and Maugham's drama, *The Letter*, the straight-driving work of a technician. In musical comedy we have to add *Oh, Kay!*, the romantic booming of *The Desert Song* (Drury Lane unable to escape from the sand), which is still being toured in 1958; and *The Vagabond King*, which began on the sturdy basis of Justin Huntly McCarthy's romantic drama *If I Were King*, and was not intended to assure us that its Villon could have written *Où sont les neiges d'antan?* or *Dame du ciel, regente terrienne.* Who cared while Derek Oldham and Winnie Melville were singing Friml's luscious "Only a Rose"? The one thing gravely false was the low comedy during which, and at all later revivals, one has begged the surcease of sleep. "Louis, old boy, it's not done!" splutters Comic Relief to King Louis when Villon is on the scaffold. (I cannot guess what H. A. Saintsbury felt about this.) *The Vagabond King* was a better musical play than *The Desert Song* which, for all its marching and countermarching, its Foreign Legion, its Harem, and its Room of the Silken Couch, had something of the emptiness of the desert. It was well that Edith Day could be in it to rule the Lane once more; she and Harry Welchman, swirling his cloak as the masked Red Shadow, saw that Sigmund Romberg's music could often excuse the libretto. These productions were in the Old Spectacular period. But it was also the season of *Hit the Deck* (New Popular) at the Hippodrome, which thundered and volleyed, with Alice Morley in "Hallelujah"; Sydney Howard and Ellen Pollock; and Stanley Holloway and Ivy Tresmand to sing the duet, "Sometimes I'm Happy":

> I never mind the rain from the skies
> If I can find the sun in your eyes.

It was the period of *Lady Luck* at a new theatre, the Carlton, that did not live long as a theatre, but had at least Leslie Henson (as a man who had inherited six widows) and Laddie Cliff to give apparent spontaneity to a first, mediocre, song-and-dance show. We had, too, the milky-mild *Peggy-Ann*, with Dorothy Dickson as a dreaming Cinderella of Daly's, and Maisie Gay in uproar; and *The Girl Friend*, adapted from something known as *Kitty's Kisses*. Hardly a night to swoon over, it has remained in the record for its Rodgers and Hart score ("Blue Room" and "Mountain Greenery"), for a fiercely grotesque dance by Emma Haig and George Gee (red-faced, marble-eyed), and for the refreshing daffodil serenity of Louise Browne. David Fairweather observed in a review: "The method of leading up to Miss Browne's dance, arranged to Tschaikowsky's *Casse Noisette* suite, is not without humour. The Bridal Suite is invaded by the ladies of the chorus. Clad in tasteful pyjamas, they call upon the bride (in nightdress and ballet shoes) for a dance. After the exhibition the ladies applaud politely, and one says: 'Thank you, dear, you dance beautifully, but you must be tired! Good-night!' *Exeunt omnes*, laughing shrilly. It must be great fun writing a musical-comedy libretto."

It is. Sandy Wilson, in our time, has proved this in his pastiche, *The Boy Friend* (a generic title). Credibly in the spirit of the Twenties, it is often accepted now—without reference to its amiably mischievous overtones—as a musical comedy in its own right. Wilson describes it as "a loving salute to those far-off days of the cloche hat and the short skirt, a Valentine from one post-war period to another", and Vida Hope insisted when directing it that it should be "witty, elegant, charming, and tender". The last two epithets might be used for *The Blue Train* which in 1927, and at a tempo unexpectedly leisured, brought Lily Elsie back to the West End stage after ten years. As gracious as ever, she returned London to the days of *The Merry Widow*. Nothing in her acting or her singing harmonised with the feverish fury of the mid-Twenties. "She dances with exquisite melancholy," said Agate, "and we reflect that Venus, unyoking at Paphos her silver doves, must have trod some such measure." We are not told how many people in the Prince of Wales's shared exactly this reflection.

A pastiche of a straight play of 1927 would be an uncanny mingle. It would have to hint at the gummy novelette-stuff of *Potiphar's Wife*, about seducing mistress and upright chauffeur; the contentious free-love argument of *The Fanatics* which, in our day, might have been a Royal Court rallying cry; and the domestic vampirism of *The Silver Cord*, acted at the St. Martin's by Lilian Braithwaite in emotional surge, and Clare Eames, from New York, with a singular clarity, almost austerity, of line. The play would have to touch on Wallace at the Lyceum, *The Terror* with weird organ music, mad laughter, "H" Ward at Dartmoor, and the Underground Chapel. It would say a word for *The Silent House*, in which Norah Robinson spent so many nights being beaten, mesmerised, tortured, and gassed. It would recall—here a successor to *The Ghost Train*—the rapt old engine-driver of *The Wrecker* who believed in "rogue engines". And it would indicate the high sincerity of Reginald Berkeley's *The White Château*, an episodic drama of the war, to which the years have been unkind. Other plays yet. In *The Garden of Eden*—my old small-town manager would have thought this just the thing—Tallulah Bankhead, for reasons best known to the author, tore off a very fine wedding dress before much of the population of the South of France. Eden Phillpotts, in *The Blue Comet*, left Yellow Sands and Little Silver to write a drama about nothing less than the impending dissolution of the world. Although the characters gathered expectantly in a Hampstead garden, it is obvious that a play about the end of the world can have no special climax if the world does not end. No dramatist can hold the Last Trump; indeed, as Edith Shackleton observed, it was all "rather a waste of a good comet".

We can see that any inclusive pastiche would be deadly hard work: a kind of Burleigh's Nod drama. It would have to remind us that Robert Loraine, nearing the end of his career, acted Adolf in Strindberg's *The Father*, a relentless night, Swedish drill for the emotions; and that he appeared also, for the last time, as Rostand's Cyrano. This was an extraordinary piece of romantic bravura. On the first night—when a fatigued stage staff at the

Apollo made error upon error—three rows of "flats", the chapel, the cloisters, and the sycamore tree in the convent garden, began to fall forward while Cyrano was dying. Loraine, said his wife in her biography, rose and straightened the sycamore, went back and straightened the cloisters, "held them up until the stage hands had time to seize them from the sides, *and yet never ceased dying.* His gestures belied his words, but his mind and his tones and his lines flowed on . . . There was not a titter, not a whisper, not a stir in the house." Loraine was an actor.

One name has been missing. We should have, of course, to add the three Noël Coward plays in a year when he discovered, so he says, on coming back from the Pacific, that he needed "every ounce of the moral and nervous stamina" that the rest had stored up in him. All at first was clear. Marie Tempest, in the Marquise Eloise de Kestournel's orange yellow and sable, and rose-speckled turquoise taffeta, was sailing through the period comedy Coward had written in America. *The Marquise*—"a pleasant little joke" he called it—was France in 1735: Marie Tempest sustained it as triumphantly as Edith Evans, in *The Beaux' Stratagem* at another theatre, was presenting the English world of thirty years earlier. To watch Eloise as she ate an orange while her lovers fought a duel for her, was to understand an actress's pleasure in her high comedy technique, and the knowledge that her quality was appreciated. Everything right there. Coward enjoyed a visit to Vienna to see a production of his play that, without his knowledge, had been transposed to modern dress: "When finally I caught the word 'Eloise' and observed Frau Bassermann enter in a red leather motor-coat, the truth dawned upon me, and I laughed so much that I nearly fell out of the box."

He felt less happy in London that autumn. A light comedy, *Home Chat*, performed too slowly before a chafing audience, was booed from gallery and pit, with a consequent, and not very helpful, exchange of discourtesies between author and objectors. Matters were worse when another comedy, *Sirocco*, which he had drafted in New York during 1921 and largely re-written, broke the sequence of musical plays at Daly's. Its scene was Northern Italy: Ivor Novello and Frances Doble had leading parts that these charming people were still too inexperienced to guide. Coward believed that the play was fairly good; Basil Dean's complicated production had an accuracy almost fanatical. But the evening was a penance: an oppressive quietness to begin, then guying from above during a love scene, and at last a third-act frenzy of yells and hooting. After the curtain there was a prolonged din. Coward "bowed and smiled my grateful thanks to the angriest uproar I had ever heard in a theatre". For seven minutes it battered on. It was after this that Frances Doble, responding tremulously to the night's only genuine applause, uttered the line born to fame: "Ladies and gentlemen, this is the happiest moment of my life."

The Cochran revue of 1927 was *One Dam Thing After Another*, among the gold and silver and azure curtains. Here Edythe Baker sat at her white piano; here Sonnie Hale and Mimi Crawford sang "My Lucky Star"; here—and from the angle of 1958, a vital memory—Jessie Matthews and Richard Dolman joined in "My Heart Stood Still". Jessie Matthews had been barely more than a child when, four years before, in a Cochran failure, *The Music Box Revue*, she sang Irving Berlin's, "I want to go back to the farm". Now London heard her in the song that belongs for ever to the Gay Twenties, Rodgers and Hart's

> I took one look at you,
> That's all I meant to do,
> But then my heart stood still.
> My feet could step and walk,
> My lips could move and talk,
> And yet my heart stood still. . . .

My provincial manager that year wanted his heart to stand still. He left during the second interval, I remember, and missed the hero's one bound to be free. The dear man would have been brighter at plays that the West End of London never saw, and that avoided our part of the country as well: *Mademoiselle from Armentières*, which kept the war on the backchat level of Privates Nobby Clark, Dusty Miller, and Spud Murphy; *She Got What She Wanted*; and *The Man and the Parson*, in which the characters were Reuben, Silas, Rosa, Little Midgy, and the Rev. Julian. Incident enough in these, I have no doubt; and there might have been something in *Out of Wedlock*, a drama in eight scenes (Hippodrome, Bury), with the Hon. Howard Naldrett, Inspector Smittle, and Dr. Phoebe Sugg.

119. Alfred Lunt and Lynn Fontanne appear together in London for the first time, in the Theatre Guild production of *Caprice*, St. James's Theatre, 1929.

120. King Magnus (Cedric Hardwicke) with "Orinthia beloved" (Edith Evans) in the interlude of Bernard Shaw's *The Apple Cart*, Queen's Theatre, 1929.

121. *Journey's End*, Savoy, 1929: Captain Stanhope (Colin Clive) insists upon censoring the letters of Second Lieutenant Raleigh (Maurice Evans).

122. "You swine, you dirty swine!": Brian Aherne and Ernest Milton in *Rope* at the Ambassadors Theatre, 1929.

123. "Come along, Wenda. Willie's getting rather restless": Owen Nares, Cathleen Nesbitt, and Gillian Lind in Edgar Wallace's *The Calendar*, Wyndham's Theatre, 1929.

124. "If Sadie be guilty—then the Chinese husband Yuan Sing may find consolation with her pure sister, Charlotte": Frances Doble and Matheson Lang in *The Chinese Bungalow* at the Duke of York's, 1929.

125. *David* (the blind composer; pretending he can see): "I can get along now. Goodbye, my dear." *Lesley:* "Don't you want me, David?" Ivor Novello and Benita Hume in *Symphony in Two Flats*, New Theatre, 1929.

X

1928

It felt far more than eight years since the decade began and Irene Vanbrugh raised her eyes from Olivia's curtains. The theatre was less stable, less gravely traditional, given more quickly to the fleeting fad. It had lost in dignity, gained in freshness. It was too ready to acknowledge Broadway, but it could think for itself, when it liked, with a defiant independence. If it missed its veteran actor-managers, it had still managements of spirit and authority besides the ever-questing idealism, variously expressed, of Sir Barry Jackson and Sir Nigel Playfair. Some great players were in the making, and producers' names were more prominent; even so, theatrical speech had seldom been so slovenly—one went now to see a play rather than to hear it. In musical comedy an ability to dance meant more than ability to sing. London continued to build new theatres—the Carlton, the Piccadilly—but they were being built without the pit: one day a famous word would have faded.

Cabaret was part of London's night-life, though the *Midnight Follies* (which had had a knife-throwing act in one of its last, post-Playfair, editions) had gone from the Metropole. Teddy Brown's Band had been at the Café de Paris since 1925; somebody called "Tiddles of New York" danced at the Queen's. In the provinces the cinema's easy conquest, and the weekly circulation of its tin boxes, had meant the theatre's recession, fewer companies on Crewe platform of a Sunday. Great holes had already been punched in the touring list, and soon the Talkies, in triumphant blare, would cause further damage. More than ever, the provinces looked to stay-at-home repertory, to such major theatres as Birmingham and Liverpool, to such weekly-change fighters as Bristol, Northampton, Plymouth, and to the seasonal stock companies, peripatetic "pomping folk", that could rough out such plays from the past as *The Heart of a Shopgirl*, *The Plaything of an Hour*, *The Blackguard of the Queen's Regiment*, and *Saturday Night in London*.

How to recapture 1928? It was the year in which a young actor, Laurence Olivier, appeared as Harold, slain at Hastings ("Sanguelac—Sanguelac—the arrow—the arrow!"), and listeners at the Royal Court Theatre, cleft between respect and mockery, heard, for the first time since Tennyson wrote his chronicle in 1876,

> . . . the ring
> Of harness and the deathful arrow sing,
> And Saxon battleaxe clang on Norman helm.
> Here rose the dragon-banner of our realm:
> Here fought, here fell, our Norman-slander'd King.

An actor three years older, John Gielgud, played with patient courage in *Holding Out the Apple* (specimen line: "You have a way of holding out the apple that positively gives me the pip"), and in *The Skull* which described itself lividly as "a comedy-mystery-thriller". There, in the setting of a deserted church in Greenwich, Connecticut, two American authors tried to get away with green lights (oddly, always green in a shocker), intermittent groans, and a coffin that rattled down a flight of stairs like Tom Walls's thunder at the Aldwych. When nothing of this came off on the first night, the management tried to get its money back by advertising "London's loudest laugh", and actually lured some people into the theatre. At the fag-end of the year Gielgud acted in *Out of the Sea*, an American drama about Cornwall that was a collector's piece in even this extremely rich and misty field ("so Celtic and quaint"). The heroine was a reincarnation of Isolde.

Donald Wolfit, down from the Sheffield Repertory company, appeared with Matheson Lang in Ashley Dukes's version of *Such Men are Dangerous*. He was Stepan, sombre, faithful serf in his red and gold uniform, who killed the mad Czar Paul at Count Pahlen's instigation. A girl of promise, Peggy Ashcroft, who would soon be establishing her reputation in Lang's cast, was then out at the Lyric, Hammersmith (her name is now gilded on the front of a stage-box), in a very small part in *A Hundred Years Old*: one of the sunnier plays of rainy Spain. Ralph Richardson was playing Shaw's other Pygmalion (*Back to Methuselah*), Gurth in *Harold*, and Tranio, a Cockney chauffeur disguised in rather too jaunty morning-coat and silk hat, in the modern-dress *Taming of the Shrew*. None of these artists would say that 1928 was a crucial year for them. Gielgud had begun to establish himself; good judges probably marked down Olivier, Wolfit, Richardson in their notebooks; but the year belonged to others.

Thus London went to see Leslie Faber, Yvonne Arnaud, and Ronald Squire as they stroked along master, maid, and man in *By Candle Light*, a comedy of impersonation, originally Viennese, that seemed at the time to be from a high heaven of wit, but is now more like last year's wafers and whipped cream. Gerald du Maurier began the spring in a second-rate drama, *S.O.S.*, with one perverse bit of casting (the Lancashire revue actress, Gracie Fields, as the troubled Lady Weir), and later startled first-nighters by playing an aged savant in the prologue of Arnold Bennett's *The Return Journey*; he spent the rest of the evening as himself in what proved to be a singularly dull modern gloss on the Faust theme. (Entry in Bennett's *Journal*, August 21: "During the morning I put down eleven titles for the play, and in the end everyone agreed on one, *The Return Journey*. Whereupon this title was officially given out to the press-agent.")

Charles Laughton had changed himself during the last few seasons into Hungarian tramp, Russian Czarist General, and American millionaire. Now he had, first, the close-cropped red hair and dead pallor of Walpole's sadist, Crispin, in *A Man With Red Hair*, unsparingly adapted by Benn Levy. Later he changed to Poirot, effervescing Belgian detective, in a treatment of a novel by Agatha Christie—who did not then write her own plays—and, finally, to Mr. Pickwick, gaiters and all, a performance more like a dry sherry than a glass of punch: Dickensians demurred. Nicholas Hannen and Marda Vanne, in Monckton Hoffe's *Many Waters*, showed what might happen during a lifetime to a perfectly matter-of-fact, but sympathetically observed, couple. Gladys Cooper, in *Excelsior* (from the French) traced the rise of a minutely trained Parisian *cocotte*. Tallulah Bankhead wore cream-and-chocolate pyjamas in *Her Cardboard Lover*. Lilian Braithwaite, Lily Elsie, and Ivor Novello were together in a light comedy, *The Truth Game*, so light that it practically vanished during performance: it was attributed to H. E. S. Davidson, "and students of the pseudonym will note that this can become 'He's David's son'": Novello soon owned up.

Hugh Wakefield, discovered on Boat Race Night upon the top of a taxi-cab at Hyde Park Corner, was involved with the dithering, finger-splicing Marion Lorne in *77 Park Lane*: one of those Walter Hackett plays that began splendidly but petered into something that might have been extemporised at rehearsal. In an earlier Hackett play of the year, *Other Men's Wives*, Marion Lorne had expressed her stage character perfectly in the words, "I am broad-minded up to a point, but beyond that I am very old-fashioned." One felt, as a rule, that a Hackett play might just as well stop at the end of its second act when the characters stiffened into a group from the canvas of some anecdotal problem-painter. Any solution would be as good as the next.

Matter more important: Frank Lawton arrived this year as the schoolboy Woodley in love with his housemaster's wife. The piece, better planned and imagined than most of the school plays that would follow it, made the name of both the actor and his dramatist, a Hampstead man of Dutch descent, then a lecturer in law at Aberystwyth. John van Druten had three plays in the West End this year, but *Young Woodley* is the one that lives: originally banned, it came to the Savoy after a club production at the Arts that converted the Censor. Van Druten was twenty-four. Just twenty-four years later, in the light of his later experiences, he wrote with wisdom of *Young Woodley* (which was able to weather the wrong type of advertisement): "I do not think it was as good as was then claimed for it, but it was surprising for me. The boys are well written. There again I was writing something that I knew, and doing a good and selective job of representation. My ear had heard them well." (He was always a listening writer, a gift many of his successors have lacked.) He added: "A critic . . . said that the sex talk was 'awkward and inhibited'. I do not think it was by the stage standards of those days." But he confessed that he failed with the schoolmaster's wife and her husband, more fictional than the other characters, and people that he had loved and hated too much: there he became literary and dangerously didactic. Still, it was a good theatrical play, in essence true. I respect it all the more after coming from a public-school play of the late Fifties, the type of anecdote that discussed "the splendours and miseries of adolescence" in a style that the late Arthur Machen, in his *Secret Glory* mood, would have received with grim amusement. I was a little surprised when a schoolboy, who had addressed his housemaster like a public meeting for what had seemed to be hours, then added: "Can I speak to you frankly for a moment, sir?" John Van Druten did it much better at the end of the Gay Twenties.

He would become an exceedingly competent dramatist of naturalism. Another writer of 1928, one whose imagination might have ranged wider than Van Druten's, was Robins Millar, a Scottish journalist. He was to be a one-play man, respected still as the author of the episodic fantasy, *Thunder in the Air*. (Its entire production within the limits insisted upon by the manager, Violet Melnotte, cost £249 9s.) In this piece a dead soldier, killed on the day before the Armistice, appeared to various people as they best remembered him. It was an idea for Barrie—very often one had to say this during the Twenties, when Barrie remained quiet—but Millar managed it more delicately than most writers would have done, and London admired the acting of Robert Haslam.

I need not say much about a play set "in a private steam dahabieh on the Nile", or of another, a version of a German comedy by Hasenclever, that ran for three performances. Nobody mentioned this when another version of the same feeble comedy, from Berlin of the mid-Twenties, tottered—a dying dodo—into the Edinburgh Festival of 1957: one of the curiosities of the stage. Another, and very successful, play of 1928, *The Trial of Mary Dugan* from New York ("Would *you* put Mary Dugan behind bars?"), also resumed its life during 1957, but here before a vast mid-week television audience*. It was discussed with passionate interest by television critics who have to go often to the theatre of thirty years ago: an experience strange to their presumably forward-looking drama colleagues, eyes ever on the day after to-morrow.

You will gather that 1928 was not very fruitful for the legitimate stage, though there are still one or two plays to recall. The musical stage had an abundant year, full of the productions that make up the fabric of the late Twenties and are now, most of them, names only, unlikely to return as either welcome revenants or tired zombies. But we do not forget how, in *Funny Face* (with the Astaires, as usual, dancing the Oompah Trot), Leslie Henson, over the punch-bowl, replied to Sydney Howard's toast, "St. George for England!" with an equally grave "King's Cross for Scotland!": two owls as solemnly drunk as ever Toby and Andrew were in the May night of Illyria. Henson's singing of "Tell your troubles to the Doc", a parody of a tired form of syncopated number, may or may not be as much forgotten as, say, "Half a Kiss" from *The Yellow Mask* (Edgar Wallace book; Chinese jewel-thieves at the Tower of London; chorus behaving like "animated ninepins"); or *The Cocoanuts*, "a snappy absurdity" from America that did not snap; or *Blue Eyes*—Bonnie Prince Charlie stuff to Kern music—in the new gold-and-green Piccadilly; or "Land of Glory and Hope Brothers", sung in *Lady Mary*

* It was revived at the Savoy Theatre during 1958.

by Herbert Mundin. This was a serene musical at Daly's, with book by Lonsdale and Hastings Turner, a visit to Australia, and a score by Szirmai. George Grossmith, as stiffly animated as ever, a galvanised lead pencil, was a personage called "Hatpin" Pinge, and round him were Helen Gilliland, Vera Bryer, and Paul Cavanagh, who meant a good deal to the Twenties, not much to us. None of these plays was inordinately successful, though all had fair runs. *So This is Love*, at the Winter Garden—a change from the heroics of *The Vagabond King*—kept Cyril Ritchard and Madge Elliott dancing for nine months. It may be thought of now merely for an idiotic scene in which Stanley Lupino, as a business man, Potty Griggs, dictated to Laddie Cliff (Hap J. Hazard) a letter to his wife. Inessentials had to be suppressed. Hence the plain statement: "Woman! I am Potty."

Memory may be happier with *Virginia* at the Palace. This was another British musical comedy. Six authors shared in it; one of the impresarios, Herbert Clayton, had a hand in the book, and Jack Waller wrote some of the music. But the setting had to be American—the Gay Twenties were in thrall—and the play survives now for its spiritual, "Roll Away Clouds", sung, with accompanying shadow-show, by cotton-pickers in their coloured frocks during a storm. George Robey, in a minor revue, again urged his audience to temper its hilarity with a modicum of reserve. A second edition of the Hulbert-Courtneidge revue *Clowns in Clover* was brightened by Miss Courtneidge's attempt to buy two dozen double damask dinner napkins. Elsie Randolph, as a woman detective, and Jack Buchanan, as himself, were encored nightly for a burlesque duet and tango, "You're the One I'm Looking For", part of an incoherent invention, *That's a Good Girl*. In a revue, *Many Happy Returns*, Mimi Crawford sang a Herbert Farjeon lyric, gravely debated at the time, "I've danced with a man who's danced with a girl who's danced with the Prince of Wales." And, at Drury Lane, Paul Robeson sang in his impressive bass a number more lasting, "Ol' Man River", with music by the prodigiously creative Jerome Kern. It has been rolling along through three decades. Certainly it bore Florenz Ziegfeld's production of *Show Boat* to success, and "Can't Help Lovin' Dat Man", Marie Burke's song, must have helped:

> Fish gotta swim; birds gotta fly,
> I gotta love one man till I die;
> Can't help lovin' dat man o'mine.

Edith Day and Cedric Hardwicke were on this voyage of the show-boat
"Cotton Blossom" down the Mississippi in the early Nineties: a voyage some
way after the Ferber novel, but original enough in the theatre to make the
previous Lane musical dramas seem wooden. Cedric Hardwicke, expert
character man though he was, could not fit into a strange world where he
had either to exaggerate or to use elaborately illustrative business. Some of
his lines, he said, baffled him; but he liked Cap'n Andy's remark (on the
change in women's dress) that the human knee was once a joint, not an
entertainment.

Two other musical plays, both boosted in their day, were dire. *Good
News*, from Broadway, glorified "co-eds". The Carlton Theatre orchestra
wore red football jerseys. The cast, with no one in it over 23, flung every song
at the audience as if it were a hand-grenade. (One lyric, "The Best Things
In Life Are Free", would have been old company for "Nothing Is For
Nothing" in 1958's *Expresso Bongo*.) The music of *Good News* was based on
the tongs and the bones; still, the West End had to surrender to the high
spirits of Zelma O'Neal, a ball of fire who led "The Varsity Drag", a kind
of demented polka. Britain replied with *Lumber Love*, a portentous Lyceum
drag advertised as a revival of British musical comedy. David Fairweather,
with his quick eye and ear for absurdity, wrote: "Practically all the songs
were introduced by the prehistoric device of dialogue-with-cue. Thus,
heroine: 'I married him under false pretences, and he hates me. My heart
is broken. What am I going to do?' Elfin boy friend (brightly): 'Never
mind, as long as *your step fits mine*, we'll dance through life together!' Song,
'Your Step and My Step.'"

Noël Coward has taken deadly pleasure in pinning this kind of nonsense.
After the horrors of his 1927, he turned 1928 unto a grand march. First, he
acted an intelligent, cynical dilettante in an artificial quartet-comedy by
S. N. Behrman, *The Second Man*. Weary and wrinkled now, it whisked along
swiftly then, under Basil Dean's direction, and Coward was in good heart
when he went to rehearsals of his one-man Cochran revue, *This Year of Grace!*
Besides writing book, lyrics, and music, he was supervising the production.
It followed that on the night the revue opened at the Pavilion, *The Second
Man*, at the Playhouse, had perhaps the fastest performance in history, so
that Coward might get across from the Embankment to Piccadilly Circus
in time for the curtain-fall. "I don't suppose," he wrote, "that a play has

ever been performed with such speed without losing coherence. We all four
rattled through it like express trains, and it was not until nearly the end of
the last act that I was suddenly conscience-stricken by the sight of a poor old
gentleman in the front row of the stalls, leaning forward with a strained
expression and his hand cupped to his ear."

The Playhouse quartet—Coward, Zena Dare, Raymond Massey, and
Ursula Jeans—duly got to the Pavilion, still in make-up, for the last
passages of a production that has endured. Everybody turned to applaud
Coward as fiercely as they had abused him for *Home Chat* and *Sirocco*. One
has only to name *This Year of Grace!* for some wanderer from the Twenties
to recall Jessie Matthews and Sonnie Hale as they sat at their lighted open
window, "A Room With a View"; Tilly Losch and Lauri Devine's formal
stained-glass window dance, "Gothic", to Bach's Air on the G String; the
romping protean clown, Maisie Gay, as she waited, parcel-heaped, balloon-
festooned, helpless, and disintegrating, by a bus stop, and billowed on as
Daisy Kipshaw, the metronomic Channel swimmer; or "Dance, Little Lady",
with all the terror of the Jazz Age in the escort of Messel-masked, robot-
dancers round Lauri Devine, the "syncopated child":

> But I know it's vain
> Trying to explain
> While there's this insane
> Music in your brain. . . .

For some there comes even more clearly the sound—the intensely aesthetic
sound—of Sonnie Hale's voice, limp with rapture. Introducing Coward's
burlesque "The Legend of the Lily of the Valley", he explains as best he can,
for he will certainly swoon when he leaves the stage, that the atmosphere of
the ballet is "definitely early eighteenth-century French, smacking of gently
undulating country life, and then again smacking ever so slightly of the de-
bauched life at court". And there is a pregnant break at "The dissolute
nobleman thereupon accompanies him to a neighbouring coppice. During
which——"

What made of 1928 a year of grace? Certainly not its crime plays. There
was one exciting entry in the crime register, A. A. Milne's *The Fourth Wall*,
which restored judgment and reason to the body-in-the-library play. We were

126. With the aid of a time-table and a telephone, Marie Tempest disposes of Ursula Jeans in *The First Mrs. Fraser*, 1929, which ran for 632 performances at the Haymarket Theatre.

127. A Disturbed Breakfast: George More O'Ferrall, Olive Blakeney, Ann Todd, Basil Foster, Reginald Gardiner, Clive Currie, and Ruth Taylor in the last act of *The Middle Watch* at the Shaftesbury Theatre, 1929.

128. The Viennese Café scene, with Norah Howard, Austin Trevor, and Peggy Wood in Coward's *Bitter-Sweet*, His Majesty's Theatre, 1929.

129. Sophie Tucker, the last of the "Red-Hot Mommas".

130. You're right—it's Dorothy Ward.

shown both the murder and the efforts of the dead man's niece and nephew to prove that it was murder indeed, not suicide. Edgar Wallace planned *The Flying Squad* on Scotland Yard-cum-Lyceum lines, and it must have been a fair cop, though no word or deed returns to me now, and Peggy O'Neil's name in the programme does not help. A better play, *The Squeaker*, contains one of the very few accurate scenes in a newspaper sub-editors' room, that chamber of horrors. *The Monster*, by an American dramatist, Crane Wilbur, smacked ever so slightly of undulating country life. It contained a maniac vivisectionist, a man without a face, an electric chair, an operation without anaesthetic, a tongueless Negro, a moving couch, and a collapsible bed. It was not much enjoyed.

Urgently, we move to other months: to the attempt by Gracie Fields, in *S.O.S.*, to play a straight, and thinly-written, part that she did as well as any efficient actress would have done it, no better; to Robert Sherwood's study of Hannibal, *The Road to Rome*—high comedy, and an attack on war—that has twice had a brief and shaky life in London; and to Elmer Rice's piece of satirical expressionism, *The Adding Machine*, with its Mr. Zero, so unflatteringly symbolic of the Little Man. ("I feared the worst for this play", recorded Arnold Bennett in surprise, "but it turned out quite well".) So did Drinkwater's *Bird in Hand,* which far outran any of its critics' prophecies, either in London—though it lost money on its year's run—or in New York. This Gloucestershire night's entertainment remained as fresh as its innkeeper's name of Greenleaf. Its speech was shaped by a writer who, like the craftsman of his own poem, "somehow moved in comely thought". Herbert Lomas, the innkeeper, used in obstinate eloquence that voice of his like a gnarled and splintering bough.

Laurence Olivier was the lover who had to mollify one of the most stubborn potential fathers-in-law in the Drama. He had had even harder work that spring when, also under Sir Barry Jackson's management, he played Tennyson's Harold at the Court. There was much strong, speakable verse in this chronicle, which began with a comet; they were popular just then in Sloane Square. "Sir Barry," as G. W. Bishop said, "had spent most of his theatrical career in giving England an idea of what a National Theatre ought to do in this country"; wisely, he let a neglected play have its chance. The company, under H. K. Ayliff, spoke it with great vigour, though Olivier might have been better ten years on; Paul Shelving's decoration suggested the

H

Bayeux Tapestry; and playgoers avoided the Court in large and increasing numbers. *Harold* was sandwiched between two of Sir Barry's modern-dress Shakespeare experiments. *Macbeth*, with its mediaeval superstition and haunted verse, did not take to khaki. Much of it was loosely spoken; Eric Maturin, the Macbeth, rasped and filed away the poetry, and Herbert Farjeon found him "the nearest thing to 'a Scottish gentleman in considerable difficulties'" he ever hoped to see. Still, it could not have been worse than a 1957 revival, by a usually sensible director, which sought "to strip off the poetical interpretation which the nineteenth-century sentimentalists put upon the plays". Hence, no doubt, the arrival of an anonymous Highland woman to sing a lament over the bodies of Lady Macduff and her son.

The Taming of the Shrew, in modern dress, came through cheerfully. After all, the play is an elaborate charade before a drunken tinker. At the Court Tranio became a chauffeur, and Grumio a Fascist, and Petruchio (Scott Sunderland) cried "Come on, i' God's name!" to the starting-handle of his rebellious Ford car. Norman Marshall, in *The Producer and the Play*, makes the point that, in an ordinary production, the contrast between Petruchio's outrageous costume and the formally-clothed guests is never as funny as Shakespeare hoped, because we do not know how an Elizabethan bridegroom *ought* to look. "The rest of the cast do their best to help by appearing to be extremely shocked, but these shocked looks had far more point and were far funnier when Petruchio, dressed in a top hat, a red handkerchief round his neck, morning coat, highly coloured pullover, a pair of khaki breeches, a riding boot on one foot and a patent leather shoe on the other, was seen against a crowd dressed with the formal correctitude of the guests at a fashionable wedding at St. George's, Hanover Square."

In the matter of modern dress I ought to record that in *The Devil's Host* (another play deep beneath the files) Adrianne Allen wore "a very rich little toilette in lime-green. The neckline runs to a low 'V' both back and front, and is encrusted with diamanté and pearl work that extends down the bodice. From the swathed Oriental hipline swing panels of a paler green—what shall we ever find to replace the subtlety given to a woman's movements by the swinging panel?" The last words have a pleasantly theatrical ring.

XI

1929

So, at last, we approach the end of the Twenties: a world darker, more anxious, than it was when the decade began,

> Masquing and humming,
> Fifing and drumming,
> Guitarring and strumming . . .

The feverish euphoria had ended; economic disaster threatened; sugar-plum romance, brittle gaiety, would turn to love on the dole. Already the world was half-way to another war. And here, exactly in the middle of the long, noisy interval, came what is still the best of the war plays, *Journey's End*, by a thirty-two-year-old insurance official, R. C. Sherriff. After eleven years we could look steadily at the grim March of 1918. Not long after *Journey's End* a single act in Sean O'Casey's *The Silver Tassie* entered the permanent collection of the English theatre.

The Stage Society presented Sherriff's play for two performances in December 1928. During the following month, under Maurice Browne, it began its West End career: 594 performances, almost as many as *The Naughty Wife*. Colin Clive was the nerve-frayed Stanhope, a part that Laurence Olivier had created; it was bad luck that set Olivier playing at soldiers in the soon obliterated Foreign Legion scribbles of *Beau Geste* when there had been this splendid chance ready for him. After we have condoned a certain amount of plot contrivance—young Raleigh, straight from school, is posted to Stanhope's company, to the hero he had worshipped—there is nothing else to forgive: the drama, piercingly direct, speaks straight to us from the British trenches before St. Quentin in March 1918.

When *Journey's End* returned in 1950, with another and a very different war in immediate history, I found its truth untouched, its invention unrusted. While the company, motionless and in shadow, took its call, I was thinking of Humbert Wolfe's line in his poem to a dead friend, "You from Givenchy [that] no years can harden." It is modish to regard *Journey's End* as an ancient monument to be examined with more or less respectful interest. But Sherriff, seeking to give no more than a firm, simple idea of the ghastly four years' tournament of the Western Front, wrote with so much honesty—no pretence, no heroics—that his play must ever stir an audience with any kind of feeling. Those figures in the St. Quentin dug-out are fixed upon the English theatre of their period, from Stanhope, with too much imagination, to Trotter, the ranker subaltern with none. We have been used, since then, to the lesser dramatist's variation upon Sherriff's theme and his characters. Always we should try to imagine the impact of *Journey's End* upon the theatre of 1929: Agate called it "a work of extraordinary quality and interest which brings one into touch with the greatest experience known to living man". When it came to the outer provinces in the autumn of 1929, those provinces where the old touring list was now in shreds and the talking cinema had begun to blaze, two young playgoers, at evening's end, walked silently by the sea for an hour before they could permit themselves to speak. That is not something to be laughed off cynically thirty years on, though nothing can seem funnier to the unemotional than emotion they do not share.

No one has laughed off the second act of *The Silver Tassie*. Startled, the Abbey, Dublin, refused O'Casey's play; but Shaw warned Lady Gregory that it would "clearly force its way upon the stage", and it did. In London, Cochran, ever ready for the new thing, presented it at the Apollo, with Charles Laughton as the Irishman who returns from Flanders paralysed from the waist downward. It is the second act that stays, the chanted choruses, the wild humours, the terror, the invocation to the gun ("Guardian of our love and hate and fear"), the entire deliberately unrealistic scene behind the lines, in the "jagged and lacerated ruin of what was once a monastery", dominated by a great howitzer. (Augustus John designed the setting.) That second act burned into the mind. Even Harley Granville-Barker, whom few would have thought in key, spoke of O'Casey's remarkable use of "symbolism of scene and character, choric rhythm of speech and movement, the insistence of rhyme, the dignity of ritual, every transcendent means available, in his endeavour to give us . . . some sense of the chaos of war". Though Laughton was physically wrong for Harry Heegan, the footballer-hero, his imagination almost overcame this. It is a terribly hard play to stage, and its writing is uneven, but the second act, if spoken and manœuvred with intelligence, is sovereign. Commercially, in that complex autumn of 1929, *The Silver Tassie* failed. Artistically, time has proved it to be anything but a failure.

This, maybe, is not work on which to end the record of the Gay Twenties. It was a curious year, graver than most, though still with a good deal of desperate escapism. The American influence was more subdued: London had tired of Broadway, except when *Porgy* put upon the stage of His Majesty's all the sound and light and heat, the quivering, storm-cast tenements, of Catfish Row, the Negro section of the Charleston waterfront. Senior British dramatists were back. Shaw had the full-voiced political extravaganza of *The Apple Cart*, which Sir Barry Jackson first staged that summer at the new Malvern Festival under the lee of those theatrical hills. Maugham's play was *The Sacred Flame*, in which he attempted "a greater elaboration of dialogue than he had been in the habit of using": dialogue deliberately, significantly formal. It did not work: those bred to Maugham's sharp naturalism were troubled when a mercy-killing mother talked of "the multitudinous stars sweeping across the blue sky of India".

Galsworthy, unluckier and unluckier, had two failures, technically similar in construction: *Exiled*, which was described as an anaemic *Skin Game*, and his last play, *The Roof*, about a fire in a small Paris hotel and the behaviour of the guests; a quiet, delicate piece that should have lived (for some a love scene between Madeleine Carroll and Eric Portman does live). Lonsdale's *Canaries Sometimes Sing* was a lesser *On Approval*, a hard, bright quartet in which partners and good lines were exchanged with swift freedom. (With the years this mirror of Mayfair would get fly-blown.) Technique called to technique when Marie Tempest, at length discovering another congenial part, acted with Henry Ainley—back to the stage after illness—in St. John Ervine's *The First Mrs. Fraser*. It was a comedy of manners by a critic-dramatist who had written finer work with less public appreciation. Compared with other plays Marie Tempest had had during the Twenties, it was bred of genius itself. Alan Dent had said of this actress, "It is in her power to strike wit out of a theorem in Euclid, to make even trigonometry scintillate," but she could not be expected to do it always.

Other technicians, "the Lunts", as people would learn to speak knowingly of Alfred Lunt and Lynn Fontanne, brought their volatile partnership to an indifferent Viennese comedy, *Caprice*. Matheson Lang renewed memories of Mr. Wu, in what we might call the melodlama of *The Chinese Bungalow* (his name now was Yuan Sing), and then went to an eighteenth-century German Duchy as Jew Süss in Ashley Dukes's version of the novel: there should be a plaque in the Duke of York's Theatre, "Here rose the star of Peggy Ashcroft." Edgar Wallace, in *The Calendar*, left Sinister Street for the Turf. The play is mildewed now, and its racing lingo tiresome: so are the people who toss about their "thousands". In those days it sounded very man-of-the-world, and one scene at least still holds: an inquiry by the Stewards of the Jockey Club (Owen Nares in difficulty). Again the theatrical year lacked any special plan. It was evident enough that portrait-plays would return to fashion. Often, during the Thirties, the stage would be on terms with the mighty dead, in the manner—if without the gleam in the eye—of the direction in Mr. Ladbroke Brown's *Savonarola*: "Enter Michael Angelo. Andrea del Sarto appears for a moment at a window. Pippa passes. Brothers of the Misericordia go by, singing a Requiem for Francesca da Rimini. Enter Boccaccio, Benvenuto Cellini, and many others, making remarks highly characteristic of themselves." The best portrait-play of 1929 had no pretensions to tushery. It was *The Lady With a Lamp*, in which Reginald Berkeley set Miss Nightingale firmly on the stage, even if the play has seemed to be less firm without an Edith Evans to conduct Florence through its mutations. Ivor Brown described Florence as "half feminine and half administrative fanatic, standing like an igneous rock among the waters of muddle and misrule".

Most of the plays that come from the hat are British. Ivor Novello, thoroughly sure of himself now as dramatist and actor (goodbye to Messrs. L'Estrange and Davidson) mixed sentiment about a blind composer with the grotesquerie of an eccentric artist, Salmon Pryde (Viola Tree) in *Symphony in Two Flats*. During a silly conversation-piece, *The Amorists*, Esmé Percy used his voice like a tortured seraph enjoying the torture. At the Aldwych the Tutts and the Ramsbothams were the neighbourly Capulets and Montagues of a Travers frisk, *A Cup of Kindness* (Mary Brough and Tom Walls at their most bristling); and in *The Middle Watch*, by Ian Hay and Stephen King-Hall, we discovered a naval variation on bedroom farce, one meant for further use. In *Rope*, with its murder for excitement, its corpse in a chest and supper on the lid, Patrick Hamilton wrote a play that made the discredited panel-school of *The Cat and the Canary* look foolish; he would go on to employ suspense more craftily than any other dramatist. *Rope*, indeed, was a lesson in the art of screw-twisting, the screw manipulated by Ernest Milton as a lame poet, sibilantly ironical, contemptuously commanding. It did better than *The Misdoings of Charley Peace*, which had seventeen changes of scene, and was advertised to begin its première at 7.59 p.m.: I doubt whether this split-second punctuality had the vaguest effect upon first-nighters.

On the musical stage it was also, largely, a British year, though the vast new Dominion in Tottenham Court Road, soon—like the Carlton—to be a cinema, opened with a golfing comedy from Broadway, *Follow Through*. Not much in this dismally jolting affair mattered except the vigour of Ada May, an American dancer: "as all over the stage," said Agate, "as a kitten is over the hearthrug or a lamb over the Botticellian field." To-day her name tinkles faintly. But we can still hear the blare, from the Gaiety, of Stanley Lupino as he sang "I Lift Up My Finger and I say Tweet Tweet, Shush Shush, Na-ow Na-ow, Come Come", in which he persuaded the entire audience, stalls to gallery, to join. Another home-made piece, *Mr. Cinders*, got Bobbie Howes (cherubic orphan) and Binnie Hale, millionaire's daughter into housemaid (again those musical-comedy caps and aprons) to sing together a not excessively original lyric:

> What's the use of worrying and feeling blue?
> When days seem long, keep smiling through,
> And spread a little happiness till dreams come true.

The House That Jack Built was a revue in which Cicely Courtneidge inspected the domestic life of Harringay; or, as the Dowager Fairy Queen, her eye like the Siddons, exploded from a blasted oak; or, as somebody's widow, renewed a former ecstasy during that will-reading smitten by laughing gas. A Cochran revue, *Wake Up and Dream*, rather fragile after *This Year of Grace!*, glistened across the Pavilion stage. Not much is left now except the rhythm of a Cole Porter number for Jessie Matthews and Sonnie Hale:

> The nightingales in the dark do it,
> Larks crazy for a lark do it,
> Let's do it,
> Let's fall in love!

Presently, and more memorably, Cochran would stage *Bitter Sweet*, its title almost a label for this last year of the Twenties. Noël Coward felt it was time for a romantic renaissance after the "endless succession of slick American Vo-do-deo-do musical farces in which the speed was fast, invention complicated, and the sentimental value negligible". Even that single-minded impresario, J. L. Sacks, seemed to have paused. A brief exchange from a 1929 *Co-Optimists* programme offers a local jest of the late Twenties: "First Actor: 'I've got a job in Joe Sacks's new revival.' Second Actor: 'What's he reviving now?' First Actor: 'The rehearsals of the revival of *The Lilac Domino*.'" Coward would get away from both the drugged solemnity of old Daly's and the clamorous helter-skelter of Broadway. One of the major musical plays of its generation quivered into life under a great horse-chestnut tree on Wimbledon Common in the early summer of 1928. Its first act was roughed out on an Atlantic voyage; Coward wrote the second in a New York nursing-home just before a minor operation; and one day, during a twenty minutes' New York traffic block, the "I'll See You Again" waltz fell into place, complete:

> I'll see you again
> Whenever Spring breaks through again . . .

The story of Sari Linden developed its final shape: its passage along the years; its core in a Viennese café of 1880 (slow curtain-fall after a tragic duel); London in the Nineties. Coward had always been able to summon a mood, and to sustain it. He would never do so more certainly than in the gas-lit café of a defiantly romantic Vienna. Later, the quartet, "Green Carnations," prickled from the Nineties:

> Faded boys, jaded boys, Womankind's
> Gift to a bulldog nation,
> In order to distinguish us from less enlightened minds,
> We all wear a green carnation.

Coward himself recalls with affection the last moment when Peggy Wood's Sari, as an old woman, straightened herself to the final chords of "I'll See You Again", and walked proudly and gallantly from the stage. *Bitter Sweet* had only a moderate London première—at first, said the author, listeners were as excited as cornflour blanc-mange—but the "operette" that various grudging notices suggested might run (with luck) for three months, moved on to 697 performances.

It had already reached some two hundred at His Majesty's when the decade ended. The last new play of any consequence in the Gay Twenties would be a farce staged on Christmas Eve at the Princes. To crumple before a Christmas audience a play must be uncommonly bad. Arthur Wimperis and Lauri Wylie's *A Warm Corner* never looked like crumpling; it had the generous broad comedy of W. H. Berry (as a corn-plaster king, with few "props" and no music) and Connie Ediss, as his wife, to send laughter ringing away towards, and into, an uncharted decade. With it, into the Thirties, went the romantic melodies of Coward, the voice of Bernard Shaw (in a revived *Pygmalion* as well as *The Apple Cart*), the singing of "I Lift Up My Finger" and "Spread a Little Happiness", and those last muffled noises from *Journey's End*: "Very faintly there comes the dull rattle of machine-guns and the fevered spatter of rifle fire."

XII

The Twenties have gone, and what remains? These pages have been starred with names and titles: too many names, too many titles, but each a fragment from the vast, ornate theatrical mosaic of the decade. Very much else lies covered beneath the weight of the years. Some of the plays in our pictures— *The Return, Plus Fours*—are nothing now but dusty acting copies on a dustier shelf. So, mercifully, is a thriller (unpictured) in which the blackmailer sent to the blackmailed "quintets of cocoa beans to call up reminiscences of old days in Africa". A summary has one of my favourite period passages:

.... It seemed fairly clear that either Hilda or her degenerate brother had had something to do with the death of their uncle, who had thus disinherited them completely in favour of Edna. They meet with some success in a plot designed to estrange Miss Darling from her Canadian lover by placing her in a compromising position, and in déshabille, with Harry, whose attempt to maltreat her is stopped in an amazing manner, presumably by Burton's confederate, just as he is half-throttled and doped with morphia from a hypodermic syringe when he is trying to hold up the Yokel, taking from the shelf a sheet of old Harding's diary bearing the bloodstained finger-prints of the murderer.

More seriously, such an excitement as Masefield's *Melloney Holtspur* (1923) can reach us now only in the text,[1] with its midnight-moon lighting, or in memories of Meggie Albanesi. What does a new generation know of, say, Ernest Milton in Pirandello's *The Mock Emperor*? Only such a note as Graham Robertson's "I have seen nothing like it since Irving".

In the cold dawn of the Thirties, John Gielgud, at the Old Vic, was just taking Shakespeare at the flood. He had acted his first Richard the Second (and worn Ernest Milton's costume) during the late autumn of 1929: in the

[1]It was, wisely, broadcast on sound-radio during the autumn of 1952.

Deposition scene, wrote his director, Harcourt Williams, "a tall willowy figure in black, surmounted by a fair head, the pale agonised face set beneath a glittering crown". His Terry voice held all the music of the word: *The Skull* and *Holding Out the Apple* were far distant. In the West End there would soon be new dramatists: Bridie, Priestley, Williams (who now remembers *Glamour*, from 1928, set in "the drawing-room of a flat over a West End theatre"?). New actors would work with brushes of comets' hair instead of with the fine stippling of a mapping-pen. The second Shakespeare Memorial Theatre was growing at Stratford-upon-Avon. The English ballet was about to rise. But all of this would belong to the Thirties: the Twenties had died.

In the dying hours of 1929 Barry Jackson and Nigel Playfair were still London managers, Cochran ruled the Pavilion, one could book for a Marie Tempest comedy, an Aldwych farce, a Leslie Henson musical play. Though the Bankhead vogue was fading, one could shout "Tallulah, you're wonderful!" (soon she would play Marguerite Gautier: "a risky do" she said with unfailing good cheer). Urgent young dramatists were as desperately "committed"—they did not use the word then—as any in 1958. New theatres were coming: the Cambridge, Prince Edward, Whitehall, Saville, Westminster. It would be absurd to cry, as Shamrayef does in *The Seagull*, "There were mighty oaks in the old days; now we see nothing but stumps." And yet honest wistfulness is no bad thing; in 1988 many may be wistful about the Fifties (choice of epithet to follow).

To-day, putting back the files and the programmes, we can think of Cochran, of whose "quiet, strange, and mysterious influence" Sean O'Casey said: "The Clowns were always on one side of Cochran, the Tragedians on the other, and he had the imaginative eye and cunning hand to weave lovely patterns round the pair of them." We think of André Charlot, big, spectacled, eager. We think of Gertrude Lawrence and her laughter; Maisie Gay—with the name that became her so well—whom illness forced from the stage; Leslie Henson's crumpled smile; Jack Buchanan's lazy zest; Grossmith and Coyne as they were on the whirling nights of *Nanette*; George Robey's reproachful commands, A. W. Baskcomb's luminous gloom, the latest "props" from W. H. Berry's basket. On the other side of the theatre were Martin-Harvey and Matheson Lang, Ainley, Tearle, Loraine and Faber, Hawtrey and Hicks; Gerald du Maurier, with his fluency, resolute chin and quick, direct glance; the lost genius of Meggie Albanesi; the legend of Mrs. Patrick Campbell (whose last West End part was Anastasia in *The Matriarch*, 1929). We think of the gash in King Street, St. James's, that was once the drawing-room theatre of London; the Alhambra, where Diaghilev had his great disappointment; the Empire, where Edith Day sang "Alice Blue Gown" and Sybil Thorndike acted Katharine before the Ricketts setting; and the Pavilion that was the heart of the Gay Twenties, "all that ever went with evening dress". Before it was transformed to a cinema in the mid-Thirties, its last-night audience honoured it as a famous music-hall and said nothing of Cochran. For some time it had been given to non-stop variety; to increase confusion, the "host" who led the last-night singing was Peter Godfrey, founder of the Gate Theatre, and, not long before, the most surprising *avant-garde* producer in Britain.

No thought of farewell darkened the last hours of 1929 at the Pavilion where they were still fresh from *This Year of Grace!* A decade later Britain would be at war again, and the lights would be out in London. But on New Year's Eve, 1929, though the interval was waning, and a sour wind sighed round the once heedless theatre of amusement, the song that beat up across the years had still the rhythm of the Gay Twenties:

> I want to be happy,
> But I won't be happy
> Till I've made *you* happy too. . . .

Ever that insistent beat; ever the crash of applause. On the Palace stage, back in the spring of 1925, Coyne looks at Binnie Hale, Hale at Coyne. Once more the song begins.

INDEX

This index is divided into two sections: PEOPLE and TITLES. References in **heavy type** are to the numbers of picture captions (*not* the page numbers). Names in *italics* are those of people and titles which occur only in the picture captions.

PEOPLE

TITLES